HAWK
comes of age

HAWK
comes of age

Published by: The Royal Air Force
Benevolent Fund Enterprises,
Building 15, RAF Fairford,
Glos GL7 4DL, England
Publishing Director: Paul A Bowen
Publishing Coordinator: Phil Coulson

Compiled & Edited: Peter R March
Assistant Editors: Gordon Bartley and Brian Strickland
Contributing Authors: Gordon Bartley, Sqn Ldr Tony Cunnane RAF, John Hutchinson,
John Oliver, Duncan Simpson and Ian Strachan
Editorial Consultant: Gordon Hodson
Photographs courtesy: Hawker Siddeley Aviation, British Aerospace,
Michael Stroud Collection and as credited
Typesetting & Design: Karin Willis
Cover photograph: British Aerospace/Geoff Lee
Cover design: Graham Finch

ISBN 1-899808-00-0

Printed in Hong Kong

CONTENTS

Foreword

The Hawk is a British success. It is the result of the dedication, enthusiasm and skills of many people co-operating and working as an effective team. At Hawker Siddeley Aviation, Kingston, an experienced design team of Hawker and ex-Folland design engineers, with an extensive background of the Hunter, Harrier and Gnat, explored, for two years, concepts of a new, advanced, jet training aircraft that was capable of development.

The team members, with skills in design, manufacture, contract negotiation, flight and ground testing, were determined to succeed. Their work was rewarded when a Ministry of Defence (Procurement Executive) competition was won with a fixed price contract for the design, manufacture, development and delivery of 176 jet trainer aircraft. Two and a half years later its first flight was achieved and after a further two and a quarter years, with the co-operation of the Ministry of Defence, Service Release was approved, on time and at specified cost.

The original ideas included the importance of a baseline for the aircraft's development. Subsequent perseverance by engineers and marketeers, demonstrations by test pilots and RAF pilots, including the *Red Arrows*, has resulted in 14 world air arms operating the Hawk today. A further development of the versatile concept is the T-45A Goshawk, a Hawk derivative, that is now in the US Navy Training System for its pilots.

It is 21 years since the Hawk's first flight and the many who have been associated with its international success can be justifiably proud of their contributions. The Hawk and its derivatives have a long future ahead and will be manufactured and operated well into the 21st century.

Gordon Hodson MBE, C Eng, FRAeS
BAe Project Director (Retired)

14 aircraft representing the countries that have purchased the Hawk. BAe/GEOFF LEE

Fully armed Hawk 100 and Hawk 200. BAe

Hawk T1 XX154 ready for its maiden flight in August 1974. HSA

US Navy T-45A Goshawk. MDC

Introduction

The most successful modern, two-seat, advanced jet trainer produced in western Europe, the British Aerospace Hawk has gone on, in its second generation, to become an equally successful weapons platform. It is 21 years since the first Hawker Siddeley Hawk took to the air from Dunsfold in the capable hands of Chief Test Pilot Duncan Simpson. The initial production aircraft for the RAF have equipped No 4 Flying Training School at RAF Valley for nearly two decades and provided an advanced flying training aircraft highly regarded by students and instructors alike.

The Hawk T1A, with its systems for weapons delivery, and Sidewinder air-to-air missiles was used very effectively by the Tactical Weapons Units at Brawdy and Chivenor and as a supplement for the UK's air defence force. Today the RAF's advanced flying, tactical weapons and navigator training at Valley is augmented by a wider use of the Hawk for target facilities flying by No 100 Squadron at RAF Finningley (soon to be RAF Leeming) and the Royal Navy's Fleet Requirements and Direction Unit at RNAS Yeovilton (moving to RNAS Culdrose in December 1995).

In the public eye the Hawk has equipped the RAF's aerobatic team the *Red Arrows*, since replacing HS Gnats in 1980. The red-painted aircraft, with their eye-catching smoke systems, have entertained airshow audiences in Britain and across Europe, North America and the Middle East on countless occasions. The team has consistently demonstrated the high qualities of the Hawk wherever they have displayed. This highly visual promotion of the aircraft has undoubtedly assisted the manufacturer in securing overseas interest and sales.

Although the original Hawk trainer was first flown 21 years ago, it is a very different aircraft that is coming from the production lines at Brough today. Not only has the performance been appreciably enhanced, but the new generation of Hawk has a state of the art cockpit and systems which equip it well for the wider roles that it now fulfils. The British Aerospace Hawk and its US counterpart the McDonnell Douglas T-54 Goshawk look set to remain in production well into the new millennium.

This book, specially produced to mark the Hawk's coming of age, outlines its evolution and development - describes some representative home and overseas operations, presents some insights from the pilots who fly the Hawk, takes a close look at each of the variants produced, lists the world-wide production, details the RAF's current fleet, and provides an outline of the key technical and performance details.

A wide range of spectacular photographs, many of which have come through the lenses of BAe photographers Geoff Lee, Phil Boyden and Chris Ryding, and Rolls-Royce photographer Peter Holman, provide the most detailed coverage of the Hawk yet assembled in one publication. Michael Stroud has generously made available the majority of the early photographs, from his extensive collection.

This book would not have been possible without the considerable effort and enthusiasm of Gordon Bartley, both for the provision of major sections of the text and many photographs. The editorial contributions from Duncan Simpson formerly Chief Test Pilot at BAe Dunsfold, John Oliver and John Hutchinson (Rolls-Royce News/Rolls-Royce Magazine), Squadron Leader Tony Cunnane (*Red Arrows'* Press Officer) and Ian Strachan (Jane's Military Training and Simulation Systems), have proved invaluable. Gordon Hodson, former BAe Project Director, has used his extensive knowledge of the Hawk from its earliest days, to comment and advise on the text and has kindly written the foreword, on behalf of the whole Hawk team.

Thanks also to the following for their assistance with the provision of detailed information for the appendices: Howard Curtis, Paul Jackson, Chris Lofting, Daniel March, Doug Revell and Michael Stroud and the contributors of the additional photographs, as credited.

Peter R March
June 1995

EVOLUTION

The BAe Hawk T1 joins the list of outstanding British jet aircraft. BAe

Since the end of World War 2, Britain has produced a series of outstanding military jet trainers, the most notable amongst these being:- the de Havilland Vampire, Gloster Meteor, Hawker Hunter, Hunting (BAC) Jet Provost and the Folland Gnat trainer. Each of these aircraft has provided valuable service to the Royal Air Force and have also been widely exported throughout the world.

To this stable of classic aircraft types, another thoroughbred must now be added – the HS 1182 Hawk. Produced initially by Hawker Siddeley, at its Kingston-upon-Thames and Dunsfold facilities, but now assembled and test flown from British Aerospace's Warton facility in Lancashire, the Hawk has evolved from an advanced jet trainer for the Royal Air Force into a world-class light combat and training aircraft. The Hawk has also provided much-needed production capacity and revenue for British Aerospace, at a time when UK defence budgets are in drastic decline – and the future of collaborative programmes, like Eurofighter 2000 and the Future Large Aircraft (FLA), remain unclear.

Ideas for a trainer/attack aircraft concept, which resulted in the Hawk, originated at Hawker Siddeley, Kingston in 1968. During the mid-1960s the RAF student pilot graduated from basic flying training on the Jet Provost to the Gnat T1 for advanced flying training. At this time the RAF's Operational Requirements Branch (ORB) was considering a replacement for the Gnat T1, that had a planned service life of ten years.

The Gnat had originated as a lightweight fighter, designed by W E W 'Teddy' Petter at Folland Aircraft, Hamble. The Bristol Siddeley Engine Company had

The evolution of the Hawk stemmed from a desire within the RAF to find a replacement for its Hawker Siddeley Gnat T1 in the 1960s. PETER R MARCH

proposed a new range of small turbojet engines of high thrust-to-weight ratio. The engine chosen for the Gnat Fighter (F1) was the Saturn. This did not materialise and the new Orpheus was subsequently selected. The lightweight fighter concept was first demonstrated with the Folland Midge, powered by a Viper 101 engine and flown for the first time in August 1954 at Boscombe Down. The slightly larger Gnat F1 prototype, powered by the Orpheus, flew for the first time from the same airfield on 18 July 1955. Both flights were made by Squadron Leader E A Tennant.

When the Gnat F1 commenced its flight test programme the Hawker Hunter was well established with the RAF and in production at Kingston and Blackpool. The Gnat concept interested the RAF and a competition was established between the Hunter and Gnat F1 for a de Havilland Venom replacement in the Middle East ground attack role. The Hunter was a clear winner and the Gnat F1 did not go into service with the RAF, but was produced and saw service with the Indian and Finnish Air Forces.

At around this time, however, Folland was successful in securing an RAF order for a new, two-seat derivative of the Gnat fighter, that would replace the Vampire T11 and Meteor T7 in the advanced flying training role. The first Gnat T1 (XM691) made its maiden flight on 31 August 1959 at Chilbolton, and 105 aircraft were subsequently produced for the RAF – the first of these entering service at CFS Little Rissington in February 1962. The Gnat T1 had provision for two crew in tandem, seated on lightweight Folland ejection seats and also featured a 30% bigger wing (with integral fuel tanks) than its predecessor, fuel tanks around the engine intakes, together with conventional flaps and ailerons. With an overall length of 31ft 9in, a wingspan of just 24ft and a maximum gross weight of 9,100lb, the Gnat T1 was highly manoeuvrable. It could achieve a maximum level speed of Mach 0.95 and a maximum Mach number in excess of 1 and had an impressive rate of climb of over 9,000ft/min.

The standard achieved by student pilots on completion of Gnat T1 training was high, but maintenance costs were excessive due to the complexities of the fuel system, longitudinal control and density of equipment installation. The Gnat's cramped cockpits, restricted visibility from the rear seat, together with its inability to sight weapons from the rear cockpit and carry an appropriate weapons load, made it unsuitable for tactical weapons training. As a consequence, student pilots completed their weapons training on the two-seat Hawker Hunter which, with its side-by-side seating, twin gyro gunsights and extensive weapons capability was an ideal training platform.

Despite its popularity with instructors and students alike, the Hunter's maintenance costs were high. A rugged and reliable aircraft, as fast as the Gnat and almost as manoeuvrable, it was powered by a Rolls-Royce Avon turbojet engine. Whilst providing excellent reserves of

The Hawker Hunter had an insatiable thirst for fuel and there was criticism of its side-by-side seating arrangement. PETER R MARCH

power it had a high fuel consumption. The Hunter's side-by-side seating arrangement was deemed, by some, to be wholly unrepresentative of the RAF's current, and projected, front-line combat types – all of which featured tandem cockpit and single-seat layouts. However, the Hunter was a trusted workhorse and was destined to remain in service, but not in the training role, long after the troublesome Gnat had been withdrawn.

In formulating AST 362 for a new advanced trainer, the ORB had been greatly influenced by aircraft developments in the United States and, in particular, by two Northrop designs. These were:- the single-seat N-156F Freedom Fighter, which had flown on 30 July 1959 and the two-seat T-38 Talon jet trainer, which had entered US Air Force service in 1961. Both aircraft were powered by two General Electric J85 reheated turbojet engines, were lightweight and capable of maximum level speeds of around Mach 1.3. It came as no surprise therefore, that AST 362 attempted to improve on the performance of these American designs. Other possible foreign contenders, subsequently evaluated by the MoD, included the Aermacchi MB326G, the Breguet/Dornier Alpha Jet and the uprated Saab 105XT.

The RAF's requirement for a new trainer looked for an improvement on this Northrop T-38 lightweight two-seater.
PETER R MARCH

For the Gnat's successor, the ORB demanded a twin-engined, two-seat aircraft, capable of attaining a maximum level speed of Mach 1.5 at altitude. In addition, the new aircraft was to be capable of operating from wet runways of 6,000ft and had to be suitable for demonstrating stall characteristics, but not necessarily spinning characteristics. Most significantly, the new aircraft was to provide the front-seat pilot with 15^0 visibility below the horizon, on approach and the rear-seat occupant with an amazing 11^0 of visibility.

Another key factor in the formulation of AST 362, was cost. Growing concern, at all levels, over the escalating cost of aircraft projects like the TSR-2 and P.1154, led to calls for greater international collaboration in the design and development of military aircraft, in an effort to reduce the burden on defence budgets and taxpayers alike. Whilst collaboration itself increases overall programme costs – when those costs are split between two or more nations, the cost burden borne by each nation is less than that of an indigenous development programme. For its part, the British Government was keen to promote collaboration with the French, particularly as, in early 1964, the French Air Force had issued a requirement, referred to as ECAT (Ecole de Combat et d'Appui Tactique). This called for a twin-engined, low-cost aircraft to replace its Ouragan and Mystere IV ground attack aircraft and its ageing Lockheed T-33 jet trainers.

The new aircraft was to be capable of Mach 0.9 at 200ft, have an operational radius of action of 500 nautical miles and to be capable of operating from unprepared surfaces, as well as conventional runways. The French Air Force was also adamant that the requirements of the training role would, in no way, compromise the performance or layout of the new aircraft. The ECAT requirement was to be fiercely contested by French industry, with Breguet, Dassault, Nord, Potez and Sud Aviation all submitting design proposals. Determined to reinforce its views on collaboration, in mid-1964, the British Government held exploratory talks with French Government officials. Representatives from the Air Staffs of both countries were also present at these talks and, later that year, were able to draw-up a Joint Operational Requirement (JOR) which brought together common elements of both AST 362 and ECAT.

In Britain, both the British Aircraft Corporation and Hawker Siddeley, had been assessing the requirements of AST 362 and ECAT and were conscious of the potential export market that could result from a successful Anglo-French collaborative agreement. In response to the AST, the British Aircraft Corporation put forward a number of variable-geometry and fixed-wing, single and twin-engined design proposals, under the designation P45. However, BAC soon abandoned the variable geometry solution as being too complex and too costly, for a medium performance jet trainer. HSA also considered variable-geometry and fixed-wing designs, in an effort to satisfy the diverse requirements of both the AST and the French ECAT, but like BAC, quickly abandoned variable geometry proposals in favour of a high-powered, lightweight, fixed-wing aircraft, capable of speeds up to Mach 1.8.

Power for the new aircraft would be provided by a single Rolls-Royce RB-153 reheated turbofan engine, or, two small Rolls-Royce RB172 turbofans. Hawker Siddeley's first proposal of March 1964, was designated SGA 153 (Supersonic Ground Attack RB153 engine), but was abandoned on the advice of Rolls-Royce who considered the RB153 to be too complex, and too costly, for a low-cost ground attack/training aircraft. They offered, in lieu, a reheated version of the RB172 turbofan engine, developing 13,000lb thrust. With its promise of considerable growth potential and modular design for ease of maintenance, the RB172 was to be the basis of Hawker Siddeley's new, and larger, HS1173 design proposal which combined true multi-role capability, with low operating costs. In March 1965, however, work on the HS1173 was abruptly terminated, when the ORB refused to consider any single-engined proposal to fulfil the terms of the AST. On 17 May

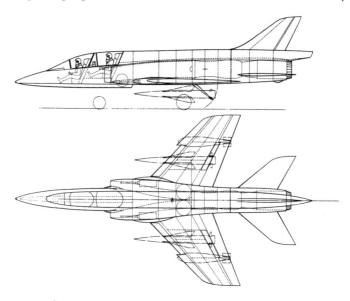

General arrangement drawings of the multi-role HS1173.
ROY BRAYBROOK

The French Air Force was seeking to replace its ageing Lockheed T-33 jet trainers. PETER R MARCH

1965, the Secretary of State for Defence, Denis Healey, announced the signing of a Memorandum of Understanding with the French Government, under the terms of which, the Breguet Br121 – the eventual winner of the French ECAT competition – would serve as the basis for a joint Anglo-French aircraft programme. The new aircraft would be powered by two small variants of the RB172, delivering roughly half the thrust of the original engine and to be known as the RT172 Adour. This new engine would also be a collaborative venture between Rolls-Royce and Turboméca of France.

Between May 1965 and November 1965, when design of the new aircraft was frozen, detailed negotiations between BAC and Breguet, led to radical changes in the Br121 design, so that it would more closely conform to the requirements of the Royal Air Force. The resulting aircraft, which we now know as the SEPECAT Jaguar, was relatively large, powerful and complex. Even before the type had entered operational service, the RAF realised that it would be an extremely costly and demanding aircraft to operate – and would also represent too great a step from the humble Jet Provost.

In 1970 the decision was taken that the Jaguar would be used solely for ground attack and operational conversion and not to replace the Gnat in the training role.

It was soon realised that the Jaguar T2 was too big and complex to follow on from the Jet Provost. PETER R MARCH

With the outcome of AST 362 decided in favour of the Breguet Br 121/Jaguar, both the British Aircraft Corporation and Hawker Siddeley turned their attention to designing a successor to the Jet Provost, with entry into service envisaged for the early 1970s. At this time, it was the RAF's intention to withdraw the Gnat from operational service by 1975 at the latest and the Jet Provost progressively thereafter. The RAF flying training syllabus would then be given over to the Bulldog for primary flying training, the new 'Basic Jet Trainer' and the Jaguar for advanced flying training. By early 1968, with extensive market surveys having been carried out by both companies, BAC embarked on a series of trainer studies under the designation P59, while for its part, Hawker Siddeley had produced seven trainer proposals under the designation HS1182.

In January 1968, the RAF's Central Flying School had produced a draft specification for a Jet Provost replacement and, by October that year, this had become the basis for Air

Staff Target (AST) 397. A further twelve months would elapse before the definitive AST was issued to industry. The CFS draft called for a medium-sized aircraft of around 10,000lb gross weight, as this would provide for greater operational flexibility and allow adequate space for a modest avionics fit. The aircraft was to have tandem seating, with the rear seat raised for enhanced visibility and, in marked contrast to AST362, a single engine. With regard to performance, the aircraft was required to demonstrate a 130kt circuit speed (100kt threshold speed), a seven minute climb to 30,000ft and a maximum level speed of 500kt at sea level and Mach 0.85 at altitude. The aircraft was to have sufficient fuel (with reserves) for a one-hour general handling sortie at sea level (1.5hr at altitude) and have underwing hardpoints to permit weapons training and/or a light ground-attack capability. The Operational Requirements Branch worked throughout 1969 to more clearly define the parameters of AST397, whilst BAC and Hawker Siddeley refined their respective designs.

The CFS's draft specification for a replacement of the Jet Provost became the basis for AST397. PETER R MARCH

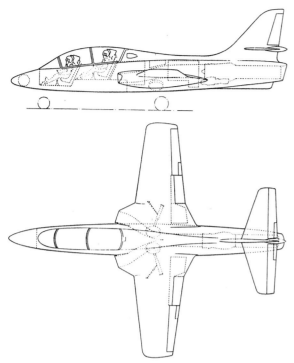

Unswept, low-wing, Adour-powered HS1182, one of 20 or so designs considered. HSA

In late 1969, both companies became aware of a change in training strategy, when the Ministry of Defence began to make reference to a new 'intermediate' jet trainer for the RAF, of which 180 would be required from 1974/5 onwards. Both companies now suspected that, whatever aircraft was selected to fulfil the requirements of AST397, it would have

to be far more than a Jet Provost replacement. Hawker Siddeley, Kingston submitted an unsolicited proposal to the Ministry of Defence in 1969. This described various possibilities for a basic/intermediate jet trainer for the Royal Air Force, that also had export potential.

It was announced early in 1970 that the two-seat Jaguar would only be used for operational conversion as it was deemed too costly and too complex for advanced flying training. With the issue of AST397 to industry, calling for a subsonic, basic/advanced jet trainer to replace the Gnat, the British Aircraft Corporation responded with its P59 proposal.

For its part, Hawker Siddeley responded initially with the Viper-powered HS1182V and then with the Adour-powered HS1182AT and -AJ, though some 20 different trainer configurations had been examined, together with 12 different engines and a variety of wing locations. The HS 1182AT was a low-cost, no frills aeroplane, while the HS 1182AJ was Hawker Siddeley's preferred solution with a close-support capability.

The BAC P59 was a tandem-seat, basic jet trainer, powered by a Rolls-Royce Viper 632 turbojet and featuring a mid-fuselage wing installation – with conventional ailerons and large Fowler flaps – intakes positioned ahead of, and slightly below, the wing leading edge and a trimming tailplane with powered elevator. With a length of 10.80m, a wingspan of 9.19m and a height of 3.64m, the P59 was similar to the S211 jet trainer of today. In determining the final P59 configuration, considerable effort

Artist's impression of the HS1182 in RAF colours, prepared in 1970. HSA

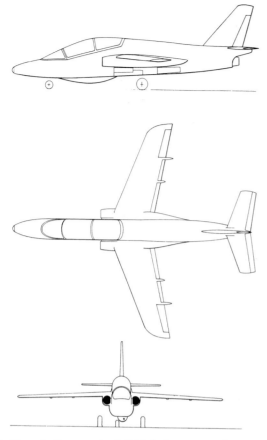

British Aircraft Corporation's P59 design proposal.

The Adour-powered HS1182 had a low-wing and shoulder-mounted intakes. HSA

was expended by BAC, in designing an aircraft with good, all-round performance, a useful weapons capability and – most importantly – docile handling characteristics on approach and landing. In producing the HS1182 designs, Hawker Siddeley had also considered a variety of configurations and a wide range of both single and twin-engine installations – at one time considering twin-SNECMA Larzac engines, as used on the Franco-German Alpha Jet trainer. Ultimately, however, the company settled for a low-wing design, with shoulder-mounted intakes, tandem-seating and a non-reheated Adour turbofan engine for fuel economy. The new twin-shaft Adour turbofan was twice the cost of the well-tried Viper. However, it was favoured by the RAF as it offered enhanced fuel economy than the older turbojet. With the 1973 fuel crisis and the ensuring escalation in fuel costs, the RAF decision proved correct.

The Adour also had a high commonality with the Adour 101 to be fitted to the Jaguar. Engine changes can be accomplished in $1\frac{1}{2}$ hours. Adour, the name given to the engine is after the river that flows past Turboméca's Tarnos factory in the Pyrenees. The design promised carefree handling in all regimes of flight, good all-round performance – including a maximum level speed of Mach 0.85 at altitude – and a realistic weapons capacity for tactical weapons training or light ground attack. From the outset, the HS1182 had been designed with exports in mind and, the decision to opt for a subsonic solution to AST397,

would clearly make the aircraft even more attractive to foreign buyers with limited defence budgets.

After detailed consideration of all submissions, on 1 October 1971, the Ministry of Defence announced the selection of the HS1182AJ project, using the un-reheated version of the Adour to fulfil the requirements of the AST which, had by now, evolved into the more definitive Air Staff Requirement (ASR)397. This ASR specified a 6,000 hour fatigue life that with a factor of five meant ground testing for 30,000 hours, a figure which had never been required for any previous RAF aircraft. Following on from this, in March 1972, Hawker Siddeley was able to celebrate the award of a fixed price contract for 176 HS1182 aircraft – there being no prototypes and production tooling was used from the beginning. The company now began the time-consuming tasks of agreeing detailed technical specifications for the new trainer and the construction of a pre-production demonstrator aircraft. The fixed-price contract defined the HS1182AJ project as Contractor Furnished Equipment (CFE), except the engine – which was Government Furnished Equipment (GFE). It was, at this stage, that the HS1182 design underwent a number of detailed changes and the configuration that resulted in the first Hawk T1 finally evolved.

The RAF refused to sanction the use of lightweight Folland/Saab Mk4GT ejection seats in the new aircraft, preferring instead to use Martin Baker seats for greater commonality with front-line combat types. This decision led to a 10in increase in fuselage length as Hawker Siddeley strove to accommodate the bulkier Martin Baker Mk10B zero/zero rocket-boosted automatic units. The RAF also requested that a Gas Turbine Starter be used to assist with airborne relights of the Adour turbofan engine, which was slow to reach idling speed during attempted relights. A number of structural changes were also made to the design at around this time, including the repositioning of the main inward-retracting undercarriage oleos, to allow an unswept rear wing spar to be incorporated. The one-piece wing is attached to the fuselage by only six bolts and has an integral fuel tank of 184 Imp gal (836 lit), which extends over most of the span. The most significant change concerned the intakes. Wind tunnel testing showed that, at speeds above Mach 0.7, the shoulder-mounted intakes of the HS1182 were causing a serious loss of longitudinal stability, due to flow separation from the intake/fuselage junction blanketing the tailplane. The problem could have been solved, but in the interests of saving time Hawker Siddeley chose the wing root intake arrangement that we see today. A Microturbo 047-Mk 2 gas turbine starter APU is installed above the Adour engine, which allows ground starting independent of ground equipment and is used for assisting airborne relights.

While Hawker Siddeley resolved the technical challenges of the HS1182 programme, the Royal Air Force had begun its search for a name for the new aircraft. Being a training aircraft, a number of university and traditional scholastic names were considered, but it was quickly realised that most of these names would be meaningless to potential export customers. A competition to name the aircraft was held among Hawker Siddeley employees and the winner was Tercel – a breed of Hawk. However, this name was not acceptable to the RAF. As the new aircraft was to be marketed as a light attack aircraft, as well as an advanced trainer, the name 'Hawk' was recommended. On 3 August 1973, that name was officially endorsed and thus emerged one of the greatest military trainers of our age.

Early overseas interest initially came from the Royal Australian Air Force, who at that time were seeking a replacement for its MB326 trainers. Eventually the Australian interest declined because of defence funding difficulties. There was also interest from the Belgian Air Force, but eventually they purchased 33 Alpha Jets.

By the spring of 1974, the first Hawk aircraft (XX154) was taking shape at Hawker Siddeley's Kingston-upon-Thames factory, with the wing, tailplane and fin assemblies produced at Brough on Humberside and rear fuselage, nose cone, canopy and windscreen from Hamble near Southampton, and the front fuselage from Kingston. The Hawk was the first British manufactured aircraft to implement the SI (metric) system of measurement. Concern was growing about whether the aircraft would be completed in time to appear at the September Farnborough Air Show. Failure to appear at the show would hand a clear marketing advantage to the Hawk's principal rival, the Franco-German Alpha Jet, which had flown in October 1973 and was scheduled to make its début at Farnborough. To save time and reduce workload on XX154, Hawker Siddeley took the decision to delay installation of a comprehensive Flight Test Instrumentation (FTI) package in the aircraft, until after the show. As a consequence, work was able to proceed at a much faster rate.

Longitudinal stability problems were overcome by having wing-root rather than shoulder engine intakes. HSA

As part of the official unveiling ceremony at Dunsfold in August 1974, XX154 was displayed for the media alongside the RAF's existing jet training aircraft – Hunter T7, Jet Provost T5 and Gnat T1. HSA

Roll-out of Hawk T1 XX154 at Dunsfold in August 1974. HSA

In the early summer of 1974, major components of the new Hawk trainer were transferred to Hawker Siddeley's test airfield at Dunsfold, where final assembly and initial flight trials were to be conducted. By mid-July, the aircraft was essentially complete and, on 12 August resplendent in a red and white gloss paint scheme, the first Hawk T1 XX154, was formally rolled out. At the time of the first flight of XX154 nine other Hawks were in the process of assembly at the Kingston works. Of these, five were scheduled for the flight development programme – the second Hawk to fly – XX157 – took to the air on 22 April 1975. XX156 should have been the second Hawk to fly but, due to the aircraft being allocated to ground resonance testing, it did not make its maiden flight until 19 May 1975. The fourth development fleet aircraft, XX158, was first flown on 1 July 1975. The two other development aircraft, XX159 and XX160, subsequently went to A&AEE Boscombe Down having first flown on 17 June and 19 November 1975, respectively.

Attention now turned to the Flight Test Department, where Chief Test Pilot, Duncan Simpson and Hawk Project Pilot, Andy Jones would assume responsibility for flying the new aircraft. With initial engine ground runs completed the first taxy trial – with Duncan Simpson at the controls – was made on 20 August, followed by two further high-speed trials on the following day. These latter trials were used to assess the engine, wheel brake characteristics and determine control characteristics up to nosewheel lift-off. Ironically, the only problem encountered during these trials was with the nosewheel which refused to centre correctly, when the Hawk was manoeuvred using differential braking. However, in spite of this problem and with poor weather forecast for 22 August, Duncan Simpson elected to go for first flight on the evening of 21 August.

The Hawk was unceremoniously towed out to the Dunsfold runway and, with all pre-flight checks completed, began its take-off roll. At 19.20hr on 21 August 1974, Hawk XX154 was airborne for the first time and a classic British trainer was born.

Duncan Simpson straps into the cockpit of XX154 during the Hawk's unveiling to the media at Dunsfold on 12 August 1974. HSA

Hawk, a new classic British jet, was airborne for the first time on 21 August 1974. HSA

HAWK AIRBORNE

A personal view from Duncan Simpson, Hawker Siddeley's Chief Test Pilot

XX154 during its first flight on 21 August 1974. HSA

In the late 1960s the Royal Air Force realised the need to replace the Gnat and Hunter, in both advanced flying and weapons training roles. They were looking for an aircraft to train pilots in all aspects of fast-jet operations, by day and night, before proceeding to their operation squadrons equipped with the Tornado, Jaguar, Phantom or Harrier.

The aircraft the RAF was seeking would have to fly well into the 21st century and satisfy a most demanding specification. Performance, handling, ease of maintenance and cost of ownership were all vital aspects of the new design, together with the ability to carry contemporary weapons in RAF training and export operational roles.

Although Hawker Siddeley at Kingston was still stretched with the Harrier and the AV-8A for the US Marine Corps, it was alive to the new requirement. Many of its staff had spent their working lives on the Hunter and they had been joined by a number of senior design engineers from Folland, who had been responsible for the Gnat. Together they formed an experienced and formidable team to design, develop and build the new aircraft for the RAF.

From 1970, the P1182 project began to take shape and proceeded through various stages in design, with close co-operation between Kingston and the RAF 'Trainers'. The first task was to win the contract for the RAF advanced and operational trainer. Dedicated effort and enthusiasm were required from both Hawker and the Ministry of Defence. With the prospect of a new British military aircraft there was no shortage of either.

The first Hawk T1 XX154 nearing completion at Kingston in June 1974. HSA

The Hawk T1 cockpit provides a comfortable working environment for both student and instructor. BAe

Duncan Simpson at the controls of XX154 before its first flight in August 1974. HSA

Gradually components of the new aircraft began to appear in the Kingston experimental department. A cockpit mock-up and installation model took shape. I visited Kingston regularly with Andy Jones and Jim Hawkins, the two project pilots, to attend design progress meetings and view progress on the aircraft, which we hoped to fly in due course. Andy and Jim were both flying and weapons instructors, with recent RAF experience, and were well aware of what was required, not only for our own service but for potential customers overseas. Endless trouble was taken to design the cockpits to give a comfortable working environment for both student and instructor with good all-round vision, modern instruments and layout of controls and equipment.

The first aircraft, XX154, took shape and confidence and enthusiasm for the project, now named the 'Hawk', increased. By the beginning of 1974 the sights were being firmly set on a début appearance at the Farnborough Air Show in September of that year. The most serious competitor, the French Alpha Jet, had already flown in October 1973 and we all knew the French would be there!

Tremendous efforts were made at Kingston, by night and day and XX154 was moved down to Dunsfold for final assembly, engine runs and systems checks in July. By early August the aeroplane was complete. When we saw it being towed round to the engine running bay we really felt that a first flight was within sight, although the days were passing too quickly for my liking.

Both Andy and I ran the engine and began to get the feel of the aeroplane, checking the systems, flying controls and our own personal equipment allied to the new Martin Baker Mk10 ejector seat. We liked what we felt. So the Hawk was cleared for flight; but first we had to carry out a series of ground runs with increasing speeds down the runway as

a final check on systems, ground handling, nosewheel lift-off speeds and test instrumentation. The tail parachute was also streamed.

First flight

The two final runway checks were completed by mid-afternoon on the 21 August and I decided to go ahead with a final briefing for a first flight that evening. The weather was good with overcast at 6,000ft and my only concern was whether the light would last for a good hour in the air. Andy Jones was to fly the chase Hunter and John Farley the two-seat Harrier and both carried photographers to record the event.

By 7.00pm I decided to go ahead and apart from the thin cloud layer, the conditions were ideal. Take-off was straightforward and we climbed out to the west to operate under Boscombe Down surveillance. The undercarriage was left in the 'down' position until the cloud layer lay

XX154 taking off from Dunsfold on the evening of 21 August 1974. HSA

below us; I levelled off to let Andy position the Hunter to record the retraction on film. All wheels locked away and the Hawk accelerated smoothly and climbed on up to 20,000ft in a clear sky with the evening sun low on the horizon. I carried out some handling checks, both with the aircraft clean and with undercarriage and flaps extended.

First impression? I was most impressed! XX154 did not feel like a prototype and, in fact, had been built as near to the intended production standard as possible, with a fully equipped and well laid out cockpit. The new Martin Baker seat was agreeably comfortable. I glanced round at the Hunter and the Harrier in close attendance and began to realise that, although we were still basking in brilliant sunshine, it was time to let down towards Dunsfold for landing. Below cloud the evening was drawing in but plenty of light for a fly-past for the few designers and builders who were watching, then into the circuit and landing.

The aircraft was inspected overnight, the records examined and preparations made to get airborne the following morning. By the end of the day two good flights had been made, the second by Andy Jones; the initial speed, altitude and g limits had all been achieved and the aeroplane remained fully serviceable.

By 28 August, nine flights had been made, sufficient to move over to Farnborough for as much rehearsal as possible. On 1 September the SBAC Show started and the Hawk flew on each of the eight days, frequently in appalling weather and remained serviceable throughout.

Hawk test pilots Duncan Simpson (left) and 'Andy' Jones pictured at the time of the early test flights. BAe

For the next two years XX154 and the other development aircraft were subjected to the most rigorous flight test programmes by Andy and Jim. The overall performance was so much better than specified or predicted. I recall the speed envelope being extended rapidly and announcing to Kingston that we would be transonic shortly. Came the reply, "Oh, we have no clearance, it is not required". "Well, get it then, and quickly, because we are about to go there!" In fact the Hawk was flown to a no limit Mach number of 1.1 true by diving it vertically from 48,000ft. It was also self-limiting to about 570kt at low altitude.

Duncan Simpson again at the controls of XX154 for its second flight on 22 August 1974. HSA

XX163 was delivered to RAF Valley on 4 November 1976 (along with XX162). ANDREW MARCH

With an 8g clearance and a full spinning and mishandling release perhaps the design team's dreams had come true! First priority, however, was to obtain service release and, due to the excellent co-operation between Kingston, Dunsfold, the Ministry of Defence (Procurement Executive) and A&AEE Boscombe Down, this was achieved to allow deliveries to commence just over two years from the first flight. On 4 November 1976 I delivered XX163 to the Royal Air Force, with the Commander-in-Chief Sir Rex Roe in the rear seat. We were welcomed at a very dark and wet RAF Valley by Group Captain David Thornton and his team of instructors.

The Hawk has come a long way since its first flight in 1974. We see it today as one of the most successful British military aeroplanes, both at home and overseas. It has proved a worthy successor to the Hunter which saw service in 22 air forces. The current Hawk 100 and 200 bear only superficial resemblance to the original T1 having been developed by British Aerospace to the highest standards of performance and equipment.

The original challenge in 1970 to design and produce an advanced trainer for the RAF has been well and truly met; it will be built and flown well into the 21st century. Those who were privileged to take part in the creation of the original Hawk will continue to watch its progress with special interest and wish British Aerospace continued success in its future plans for this remarkable aircraft.

Duncan Simpson

Development Flying

With the maiden flight of Hawk XX154 successfully completed on the evening of 21 August 1974, the Flight Test Department, at Dunsfold, then turned its attention to accumulating sufficient experience with the aircraft, for it to appear in the flying display at Farnborough. Two further flights were made on 22 August – one by Duncan Simpson, the other by Andy Jones, which extended the aircraft's flight envelope to 400kt IAS and 0.8 IMN (Indicated Mach Number). By the evening of 28 August, nine flights had been completed.

XX154's tenth flight was to Farnborough on 29 August, in readiness for the Press Preview on Sunday 1 September. Its arrival must have come as an unwelcome surprise to both Dassault and Dornier who, up to then, believed that

XX154 landing at Farnborough, making its public début in September 1974. PETER R MARCH

The first Hawk XX154, along with XX157 that first flew in April 1975. HSA

their new Alpha Jet would have the advanced jet trainer field at Farnborough to itself. Throughout the show, XX154's daily flight routine was restricted to gentle manoeuvres only, although at times, the aircraft had to

The first four development Hawks (XX154, XX156, XX157 and XX158) carrying 1, 2, 3 and 4 respectively on their fins. HSA

contend with some appalling wet and windy weather conditions. The Hawk acquitted itself well, before the critical gaze of a truly international audience and attracted considerable interest from the world's media and foreign buyers alike. By the time that the Farnborough show was over and the initial flight trials had been completed on 11 September, the Hawk had accumulated 17.5 flying hours in 26 flights. Throughout this period, the aircraft and its Adour engine had been totally reliable.

XX154 continued the comprehensive flight test instrumentation until 19 December 1974. As a result of the initial flying, two modifications were made to the flying control system. Linear gearing in the ailerons control circuit was fitted – mainly to give better lateral control response. Flight testing then began in earnest. As Hawk production built up, XX154 was joined by the first five production aircraft, XX156-XX160. XX154 and XX156 were in due course, refurbished and handed over to the Ministry of Defence (Procurement Executive).

Problems encountered during the flight test programme were relatively few. No single problem could be regarded as

Hawk T1 XX156 shows the revised fairing at the base of the rudder that was introduced early in the flight test programme to improve directional stability. PETER R MARCH

a serious threat to the safe operation of the aircraft. Early Hawk flight development flying was to concentrate on fine-tuning the controls for more positive response; on improving directional stability, wing stall characteristics and stall warning. An abrupt nose-down trim change at high speed when the airbrake was extended, was also

subject to investigation. Fixing these problems, led to minor changes to the Hawk wing and rear fuselage but, as a consequence, handling characteristics were significantly improved.

The introduction of the rudder centring spring improved directional characteristics. Further improvement was made by changing the ventral strakes under the rear fuselage and adding a fairing, extending aft, at the base of the rudder. This fairing was affectionately known as 'Fred's Rear End', after Fred Sutton who was Head of Flight Test Services at Dunsfold and suggested the change.

The stall and stall warning were investigated by photographing tufts on the wing. Wing drop was too severe at the stall and warning was insufficient. An acceptable standard was achieved by removing the inboard fence and locating a larger fence outboard to control airflow across the wing and adding two triangular leading edge 'breaker' strips on each wing.

Later in the programme a characteristic was discovered by Duncan Simpson, whilst investigating the stall at high altitudes, where the tailplane could become stalled with flaps extended and undercarriage retracted. This was due to

Hawk T1 XX156 carried out hot weather trials from RAF Luqa, Malta in June 1975. HSA

XX157 carrying Matra 155 rocket pods and a 30mm Aden gun pod on the centreline, in 1976. HSA

downwash from the double slotted flaps affecting the airflow over the tailplane. The solution was to delete one-sixth of the flap vane span which removed the effects of downwash on the tailplane.

The nose-down trim change, on airbrake selection, was found to result from a combination of airbrake deployment speed and the positioning of two small strakes on the airbrake. Taken together, these two factors seriously disrupted airflow around the lower rear fuselage and tailplane. The problem was resolved by making airbrake deployment more progressive, using a restrictor in the hydraulic system and by removing the small strakes from the airbrake. These were enlarged and repositioned on the rear fuselage either side of the airbrake to improve the directional characteristics.

Warm weather trials were carried out in XX156 at RAF Luqa in Malta during June 1975 when 15 trials sorties were flown. Performance of the aircraft, engine and systems were recorded during representative sortie conditions. During the Malta trials XX156 was flown with maximum external stores configuration on four pylons, together with a centreline gun installation. From Malta, XX156 flew to Egypt to give ten demonstration flights to the Egyptian Air Force – who, at that time, was a potential customer for the Hawk.

Flight testing of the Adour engine was virtually trouble-free, except for a vibration during high-level cruise. This problem could worry student pilots, even if it presented no real danger to the aircraft. The problem was ultimately diagnosed with the assistance of the Royal Aircraft Establishment at Farnborough, who found that longitudinal pulsing of the low pressure spool (LPS), within the engine, was transmitted to the airframe as a vibration, which in turn, was felt in the cockpit as a high frequency buzz. Rolls-Royce acted quickly to resolve the matter by introducing spring-loading of the LPS, to give it positive, uni-directional loading.

Duncan Simpson and Andy Jones took the Hawk to the Paris airshow at Le Bourget in June 1975, where the aerobatic qualities of the Hawk were demonstrated before the public for the first time. As at Farnborough the previous September the Hawk was competing head-on against the Alpha Jet. At the Farnborough show in 1976 XX154 was able to fully display in front of the British public. On this occasion a team, led by Duncan Simpson, flew nine Hawks in an immaculate close arrowhead formation in the flying programme. The leading Hawk, XX156 was painted in RAF camouflage and was fitted with fuel tanks on the inboard pylons and Sidewinders on the outer pylons. This was the first time that a Hawk had appeared in public carrying such external stores. ZA101/G-HAWK, the company-funded Hawk T1 demonstrator painted in a duo-tone desert brown camouflage was immediately behind XX156. The remainder of the formation was seven Hawks finished in the red and white colour scheme of RAF trainers. These aircraft were flown by Hawker Siddeley, RAF and Boscombe Down pilots – two of which were American pilots on exchange with the RAF.

ZA101/G-HAWK was the first Hawk to appear in public with armament at the 1976 Farnborough airshow. BAe

As flight testing had progressed, so too had the weapon clearance programme. By late-1976, the 30mm Aden gun pod, Matra 155 Rocket Pod and the CBLS (Carrier Bomb Light Store) unit, had all been successfully tested on the Hawk. With initial CA (Controller Aircraft) Release granted in October 1976, the way was clear for Hawker Siddeley to begin deliveries to an eager Royal Air Force.

The Hawk was gradually delivered into RAF service. Four units initially received the new trainer – RAF Valley for advanced flying training, RAF Brawdy and RAF Chivenor for tactical weapons training and the RAF aerobatic team – the *Red Arrows* at RAF Kemble.

By late 1976 the Hawk had been cleared to carry the Matra 155 rocket pod (starboard pylon), a CBLS (practice bomb carrier) (port pylon) and the Aden 30mm gun pod carried here on the fuselage centreline. BAe

The 'scratch' team of Hawks that appeared at the 1976 Farnborough display. The formation is led by Duncan Simpson in XX156 carrying sidewinders and drop tanks, followed by G–HAWK in desert camouglage. HSA

INTO SERVICE

Carrying the CFS badge on its tail, this Hawk was first used to train instructors at RAF Valley. BAe

The Hawk T1 flight test programme, centred on Hawker Siddeley's development airfield at Dunsfold, Surrey, uncovered few problems with the aircraft and none that could be regarded as a serious threat to its safe and effective operation. As a consequence, just over two years after its maiden flight, the Hawk was granted the initial Controller of Aircraft Release to Service in October 1976. The way was now open for the new advanced jet trainer to begin its long and distinguished career with the Royal Air Force.

With the arrival of two Hawk T1s (XX162 and XX163) at RAF Valley on 4 November 1976, a whole new era of flying training began. The first few aircraft were utilised by a detachment of the Central Flying School at the station to train the instructors for No 4 Flying Training School (FTS). It was not until the early summer of 1977 that the first student pilots began training on the Hawk. Their Advanced Flying Training (AFT) course then covered 22 weeks and involved 75 hours of dual and solo flying, supplemented by 21 hours of tuition on the Hawk flight simulator. The first Hawk-trained student pilots graduated from No 4 FTS on 11 November 1977, just days before the station took delivery of its final aircraft from the initial batch of 25.

From January 1978, Hawk deliveries switched to RAF Brawdy and by June of that year 26 Hawk T1s were operational with No 1 Tactical Weapons Unit (TWU). The first graduates from Valley moved to Brawdy in the spring of 1978 and ultimately became the first Hawk-trained TWU graduates. Their course lasted 16 weeks, during which time they flew 64 sorties, comprising 18 hours dual instruction and 36 hours solo. As new Hawk aircraft arrived at Brawdy, so the resident single and two-seat Hunters were phased

A trio of Hawks (XX164/CFS, XX166/4FTS and XX170/4FTS) flying from RAF Valley. BAe

Line-up of Hawks at Valley, including the last aircraft (XX185) of the initial delivery batch. BAe

out, with the final aircraft departing in September 1979, a year earlier than had been planned.

Nine modified Hawk T1s were delivered to RAF Kemble in 1979 for use by the RAF aerobatic team – The *Red Arrows*, that was still flying the Gnat through the 1979 display season. These Hawks, painted in the team's distinctive red colour scheme, incorporated modifications to the fuel system of the Adour turbofan engine allowing a more rapid throttle response. On the fuselage centreline they carried a 70 Imp gallon smoke pod containing separate

Hawks replaced Hunters with No 1 Tactical Weapons Unit at Brawdy from January 1978. BAe

The RAF Red Arrows *received red-painted Hawks to replace* Gnats *in 1979.* PETER R MARCH

Coloured smoke is generated by adding red or blue dye into the diesel oil that is fed into the jet eflux. PETER R MARCH

tank compartments for diesel oil and red and blue dye. When fed into the hot jet eflux, the diesel on its own creates white smoke, whilst injecting red or blue dye creates red or blue smoke. The *Arrows* gave the first Hawk display at RAF Kemble in November 1979 before invited members of the press, but it was not until April 1980 that the team gave its first public displays. Since then, the team has displayed all over the world and has been a potent force in the promotion and marketing of the Hawk.

The RAF took delivery of its 176th, and final new-build Hawk (XX353), on 9 February 1982, but the honour of being the final Hawk delivered must go to XX158. It was one of the early flight development airframes which, having been totally refurbished by British Aerospace, was delivered to RAF Chivenor on 17 March 1982.

The 176th and final new-build Hawk (XX353) delivered to the RAF on 9 February 1982. ANDREW MARCH

Modified to carry AIM-9 Sidewinder air-to-air missiles – these Hawk T1As were flown by Nos 63 and 151 'Shadow' Squadrons at RAF Chivenor for close air defence. BAe

Expectations Fulfilled

In its 21-year career, the Hawk has fulfilled – and in many cases exceeded – the objectives of the design team. The aircraft has proved to be safe, rugged, reliable and highly adaptable and to date has over 600,000 flying hours with the RAF. Of the 176 Hawk T1/1As delivered to the RAF, just 28 have been lost in accidents – a figure well below the originally projected attrition rate of 0.6 aircraft per 10,000 flying hours. Few serious technical problems have been experienced with the Hawk, although more recently certain aircraft began to experience fatigue cracking in the wings and tailplane. The problems were confined to older aircraft operating in the punishing, high-speed, low-level, tactical weapons training environment. In 1989 the RAF, in conjunction with British Aerospace, began a wing replacement programme to extend the planned life and, by 1993, 83 aircraft had been suitably modified. Work on a second batch of 59 aircraft began in November 1993, and by June 1995 this programme had been completed.

As for adaptability and mission flexibility, the Hawk's service record speaks for itself. Having begun life as an advanced flying and weapons training aircraft, it was soon

Hawk T1A (No 234 'Shadow' Squadron), an element of No 1 TWU at Brawdy, flying with a Tornado F3 on a mixed fighter force air defence exercise. BAe

The Red Arrows' *Hawks were included in the T1A modification programme. Here, one of the team's aircraft is carrying the centreline gun pod and AIM-9 Sidewinders.* BAe

adapted for display flying with the *Red Arrows*. In addition to its tactical weapons training role, the TWU Hawks were given a front-line role and allocated to 'shadow squadrons' that would, in times of crisis, be capable of carrying out limited combat missions. Originally, the aircraft operated restricted ground attack missions but the decision was taken in 1980 to extend this role to include a limited air defence capability. Between 1983 and 1986, 88 Hawk T1s, including the aircraft flown by the *Red Arrows*, were modified by British Aerospace to carry AIM-9 Sidewinder air-to-air missiles, for close air defence of vital assets such as airfields and radar installations. These modified aircraft were subsequently redesignated as Hawk T1As and all, except the *Red Arrows'* machines, were repainted in the standard RAF air defence light grey scheme.

Over the last five years, cuts in defence spending have progressively brought about a sharp reduction in the RAF's requirement for pilot training. Since 1 October 1994 there has been just one fixed wing advanced flying training

Representing each of the squadrons of No 4 FTS: XX190 – No 74(R) Sqn, XX239 – No 19(R) Sqn and XX290 – No 234(R) Sqn. BAe

school, No 4 FTS at Valley, which takes the student from BFT into AFT and on through the tactical weapons training ready to join an Operational Conversion Unit (OCU). The FTS is equipped with 72 Hawk T1/1As that are operated by Nos 19(Reserve), 74(Reserve) and 208(Reserve) Squadrons. The training of instructors continues at Valley. The FTS will be joined later this year by a further nine Hawks when the fast jet navigator training element of No 6 FTS moves in from RAF Finningley. No 100 Squadron is equipped with 16 Hawk TI/1As for its target towing and radar target tasks. Although currently based at RAF Finningley, this squadron is relocating to RAF Leeming in the latter part of 1995. Other Hawk T1/1A operators include the Institute of Aviation Medicine (IAM), the Empire Test Pilots School (ETPS) at Boscombe Down, RAF St Athan Station Flight and the Defence Research Agency (DRA). From late-1994 the Royal Navy received redundant RAF Hawks to replace its Hunters with the Fleet Requirements and Direction Unit (FRADU) at RNAS Yeovilton.

From September 1991 Hawks replaced Canberra TT18s for target facility and banner towing with No 100 Squadron. The unit is moving to RAF Leeming in 1995. BAe

The RN Fleet Requirements and Direction Unit (FRADU) had replaced its Hunters with ex-RAF Hawks by March 1995. FRADU is moving from RNAS Yeovilton to RNAS Culdrose in December 1995. BAe/PHIL BOYDEN

ETPS

Three Hawk T1s (XX341, XX342 and XX343) were delivered new, as standard aircraft, to the Empire Test Pilots' School (ETPS) at Boscombe Down in mid-1981. One aircraft (XX341) was converted as the ASTRA variable

The Empire Test Pilots School's variable stability (ASTRA) Hawk.

PETER R MARCH

stability aircraft. This variable stability system Hawk has been modified with a fly-by-wire control system, head-up display and both centre and side-stick controllers. The ASTRA Hawk was designed and developed by the Cranfield Institute of Technology in 1986 to replace the long-serving Beagle Basset variable stability aircraft. Whilst in flight the instructor can introduce changes in the aircraft parameters and alter the feel of the stick. Its handling characteristics can be varied over a wide envelope and simulate a variety of stability and control characteristics using a digital computer and autopilot actuators. The Hawk is invaluable for demonstrating the theory taught in the Ground School without the constraints of the relatively conventional handling qualities of other aircraft in the fleet.

Students have inverted spinning included in their syllabus. Until recently these manoeuvres were taught exclusively on the Hawker Hunter T7, but with its retirement this training has now to be done on the Hawk. Although the Hawk has a natural reluctance to spin it has now received clearance to perform inverted spin training. The other two ETPS Hawk T1s are fully instrumented and used for handling and performance assessments.

ETPS Hawks (XX342 and XX343) are used for handling and performance assessments, including inverted spinning.
PETER R MARCH

Externally the ETPS aircraft look very similar to the standard RAF T1s. On closer examination an airstream direction detector is mounted on the pitot head and there is an outside air temperature probe on the port side of the nose. In the cockpit there are more significant changes. A visual indicator package is located across the top of the instrument panel coaming. The instrumentation includes control positions and forces displays, angle of attack and sideslip displays and a relocated stopwatch. An extra UHF set is installed to give provision for a telemetry communications frequency. A modular data acquisition system (MODAS) is fitted to record various aircraft parameters.

Pilot's Perspective

Aerodynamic refinements made to the Hawk, during its flight test and development programme, resulted in an outstanding advanced flying and weapons training aircraft, that does not make too many demands on its pilot, but is still challenging to fly well. Carefree handling characteristics in all regimes of flight, adequate reserves of power, and almost miserly fuel consumption, make the Hawk a valuable training asset for the Royal Air Force. Since the type entered service in November 1976, hundreds of aircrew have completed their advanced training on the Hawk. Almost to a man (and woman), they have nothing but praise for the aircraft.

Operating the Hawk holds few surprises for the student pilot. Having completed his external 'walk round' checks, the pilot climbs into the cockpit and proceeds to strap in. Having checked around the cockpit, from left to right, he then starts the gas turbine starter (GTS), which provides high pressure air to turn the engine, during the start-up sequence. At start-up, engine rpm is allowed to reach 15%, before the high pressure fuel cock is opened for engine light up. Once idling rpm is reached, the GTS shuts down automatically. Engine-related temperatures and pressures are then checked, along with the operation of cockpit instruments. Primary flight controls are checked for full and free movement.

With taxi clearance given, power is increased and brakes are released, to be re-applied almost immediately, to check for satisfactory operation. The aircraft now taxies to the runway holding point. Control of the Hawk on the ground is effected through a fully-castoring nosewheel and differential toe-braking, which does take a little time to master effectively. At the runway holding point, brakes are applied and final pre-flight checks, again from left to right around the cockpit, are completed. Full and free movement of flying controls and flaps is re-checked and cockpit canopy and seat harnesses are checked for security. With take-off clearance given, the Hawk moves onto the active runway and lines up on the runway centreline, a short distance ahead of the threshold markings. Brakes are re-applied.

As full power is selected, brakes are released, and the Hawk accelerates rapidly down the runway, its wide track undercarriage providing considerable directional stability. At around 50kt, the rudder becomes effective and provides additional directional stability until, at around 90kt, slight back pressure on the control stick raises the nosewheel off the runway. At 120kt, the Hawk finally becomes airborne

Access to the Hawk's cockpit is easy. PETER R MARCH

The nosewheel lifts off when the stick is eased back at about 90kt.

Undercarriage retracted, the climb angle is reduced to six degrees.

In the circuit it all happens very quickly. PETER R MARCH

and a climb angle of eight degrees is selected. Once the undercarriage has been retracted, the climb angle is reduced to six degrees. The Hawk accelerates rapidly to 350kt, at which point, the optimum climb angle of 11 degrees is selected. Within ten minutes of take-off, the Hawk can attain altitudes in excess of 40,000ft.

At high altitude, the Hawk is somewhat limited in power, but still retains adequate margins of performance to allow the demonstration of compressibility effects, and the problems associated with maximum rate manoeuvring. At altitudes of around 40,000ft, the fuel consumption of the Hawk T1's Adour Mk 151 turbofan engine is almost miserly, so altitudes such as these are normally selected for sorties requiring long range and endurance. In these situations, aircraft speed can vary between 270kt and 160kt, depending on the sortie profile.

At medium altitude, the Hawk handles superbly and an extensive range of aerobatic manoeuvres can be demonstrated, including inverted flight. The pilot must, however, pay particular attention to engine power settings, in order to avoid over-stressing the airframe or causing the

engine to flameout, through extreme manoeuvring at low speed. Stalling can be demonstrated with the Hawk, as it is normally quite docile, with adequate warning of the onset of the stall. Recovery is almost instantaneous, once back pressure on the control stick is released. Spinning too can be demonstrated, but requires positive control inputs to overcome the aircraft's natural reluctance to spin. Spinning characteristics can vary but, in all cases, recovery is effected by centralising the controls.

At low level, the Hawk T1 can comfortably operate at speeds of up to 500kt and is highly manoeuvrable. However, the aircraft's wing loading makes it susceptible to turbulence, and this can lead to a bumpy ride.

In the circuit, events happen quickly. The initial downwind leg is flown at 190kt, with speed decaying to 150kt as the aircraft is turned on to base leg. Turning on to final approach, speed decays to 130kt, with a target speed of 110kt (plus 1kt for every 100kg of fuel remaining). For the approach, a minimum power setting of 70% is always selected to minimise engine response time, should an overshoot be necessary. Because of its twin-spool design, the Adour engine is relatively slow to accelerate and flight idle to full power can take as long as eight seconds.

The engine's response time also impacts upon formation flying and pilots of the Hawk T1 must learn to anticipate power settings, for accurate station keeping. In the case of the *Red Arrows* aircraft, the situation has been improved through modifications to the Adour engine, improving acceleration time to five or six seconds. If an overshoot is initiated, selection of full power, combined with a mid-flap setting, provides huge quantities of lift and the Hawk streaks heavenward, with an excellent rate of climb.

To get a balanced view of the handling qualities of the Hawk T1/1A, we once again turned to RAF Valley and were able to discuss the aircraft with Squadron Leader D A (Andy) Wyatt, Deputy Chief Instructor, with over 2,400 hours experience on the Hawk and Flying Officer Andy Challen, a student pilot with just over 40 hours on the type.

Low-level and high-speed, the Hawk's ride is somewhat bumpy.
PETER R MARCH

The Hawk handles superbly through a wide range of aerobatic manoeuvres. BAe/GEOFF LEE

The Hawk's tandem seating and views from the rear cockpit are excellent for student and instructor alike. BAe

Andy Wyatt's first contact with the Hawk, was as a student pilot, at RAF Valley in 1981 but, since then, he has instructed on the type at both RAF Chivenor and RAF Valley. He has also spent three years with the *Red Arrows*, first as 'Red 8' and then as one of the Synchro Pair. His experience of the aircraft is wide-ranging and takes in advanced flying training, weapons training and formation display flying. He described the Hawk as "a big step-up from the JP5 (Jet Provost T5) – particularly in terms of speed... and the tandem cockpit layout really gives you the impression of being on your own in a single-seat aeroplane. Ergonomically, the aircraft was a magnificent step-up from the Jet Provost, with a well laid-out cockpit, where everything fell nicely to hand". Positive aspects of the Hawk, emphasised by Andy Wyatt, were the aircraft's outstanding manoeuvrability; the exceptional visibility from the rear cockpit and the fuel economy of the Adour engine – particularly at altitude. On the negative side, however, he disliked the cockpit windscreen arch – which creates an obstruction during formation flying and low-level tactical weapons training. The aircraft's high-speed, low-level ride,

he described as bumpy. Asked what he would like to see in any future Hawk replacement, Andy Wyatt replied "a one-piece F-16 style canopy; a more powerful engine – such as the Adour 871 – and more digital avionics, such as multi-purpose displays".

For a newcomers view of the Hawk T1/1A, we then talked to Flying Officer Andy Challen of No 208(R) Squadron, who had arrived at RAF Valley in the summer of 1994, following a refresher course on the Shorts Tucano at the Royal Air Force College, Cranwell. Andy Challen had also undertaken his basic flying training on the Tucano and was therefore able to provide a useful comparison of the Hawk and Tucano. His first impression of the Hawk was "the speed – with the Hawk, events happened so much faster. With the Tucano, at low-level, you are covering roughly four miles per minute whereas with the Hawk, it is over seven miles per minute". Positive aspects of the Hawk when compared to the Tucano were, according to Andy Challen, the extra reserves of power on the Hawk; superior cockpit visibility; a smoother and quieter ride; more responsive controls and better emergency controls. On the negative side, he was critical of the Hawk's cockpit windscreen arch; engine response time in the circuit and the layout of the VHF/UHF radios. Asked what he would like to see in any future Hawk replacement, his views echoed those of Squadron Leader Wyatt – "greater cockpit visibility – particularly from the front cockpit; more power – especially when carrying external stores, and a more modern 'glass' cockpit".

The wide windscreen arch restricts the pilot's view for low-level tactical and formation flying. PETER R MARCH

The Hawk 100's 'glass' cockpit would be a welcome feature of future RAF Hawks. BAe

BUILT TO LAST

The Hawk has shown outstanding operational reliability. RICK BREWELL

The good handling characteristics of the Hawk T1 and other export variants of Hawk have been convincingly, and expertly, demonstrated to the world at large by the *Red Arrows* aerobatic team and British Aerospace test pilots. Many people still assume that the Hawk's performance in the air is solely responsible for its operational success with the Royal Air Force – and 14 air arms around the world. However, there is much more to it than that.

Equally important factors in the aircraft's success are the simplicity and durability of the Hawk's airframe, its operational reliability and its low cost maintenance. When you add these to true mission flexibility and the low fuel consumption of the Adour turbofan engine, you have a recipe for long-term export success. While many people appreciate the outstanding flying characteristics of the Hawk, few people appreciate the detailed technical aspects of the aeroplane, or the design philosophy behind it.

Designed in the late-1960s/early 1970s and first flown in August 1974, the Hawk embraces proven materials

technology and traditional manufacturing techniques. This has resulted in a rugged airframe that is not only extremely reliable, but also requires only the most basic technical skills to maintain. For a better understanding of the technicalities of the Hawk, a brief analysis of the Hawk T1, provides a good starting point.

From an engineering viewpoint, the RAF's Hawk T1 is a robust and uncomplicated design. The aircraft structure is manufactured from aluminium alloy sheets, extrusions and machined components, with a small amount of steel for highly-loaded components. Some magnesium alloy is used in the interests of saving weight. The aircraft fuselage is of simple aluminium skin, stringer and frame construction. It has provision for the tandem cockpit, the engine, flying control systems and services, together with a large bag tank holding 185 Imp gal (840 litres) of fuel. There is a large cut-out in the lower fuselage for the wing and, to the rear, the hydraulically-operated airbrake. The wing is moderately swept and built in one piece. Ailerons and slotted flaps are

RAF Hawk T1 production line at Dunsfold in 1978. BAe

mounted on the trailing edge of the wing. The forward fuselage ahead of the cockpit houses some of the standard avionic equipment and the forward-retracting, single wheel, nose oleo assembly.

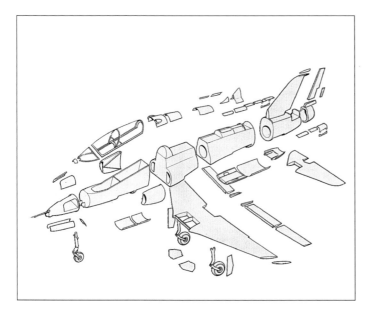

Hawk T1 manufacturing breakdown. BAe

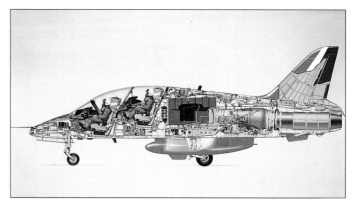

The RAF's Hawk T1 is a robust and uncomplicated design. BAe

The aircraft cockpit, which is fully-pressurised and air conditioned, accommodates the two crew in tandem, seated on Martin Baker Mk 10B, zero-zero ejection seats (basically similar to that used in the Tornado), beneath a sideways-hinging, single piece canopy which incorporates integral Miniature Detonating Cord (MDC). The canopy is of single curvature thus providing good visibility. Should ejection be necessary, the MDC breaks the canopy as seat movement is initiated, to reduce the time taken for the crew to escape. The rear cockpit is raised to provide the flying instructor with an exceptional field of view, thus enabling him to monitor the actions of the student and see the touchdown point during landing. Instruments, in both the front and rear cockpits are of the analogue (clocks and dials) type,

From the raised rear seat the instructor has a good view forward, beneath the single curvature canopy with its integral miniature detonating cord. BAe

The crew is accommodated in tandem with a sideways-hinging, one-piece canopy. PETER R MARCH

The T1's cockpit layout is conventional for the period of its initial design. BAe

and traditional lever-type switches are employed throughout. For weapon aiming, Ferranti ISIS weapon aiming sights are also incorporated. Both cockpits are supplied with gaseous oxygen from two, 1400 litre cylinders mounted behind the rear seat frame. A 70 litre emergency oxygen bottle is also located on the back of each ejection seat. The oxygen system provides a flight duration of approximately four hours on 'airmix' for the two crew.

The Hawk T1's low-set, one-piece wing with two main spars includes hydraulically operated ailerons, double-slotted flaps, an integral fuel tank and the main undercarriage oleo units, which are capable of absorbing sink rates in excess of three metres per second. The wing has attachments for four weapons pylons, although the Royal Air Force elects to utilise only two. The wing consists of aluminium alloy ribs and machined, aluminium alloy, wing skins, with integral stringers. The swept tailplane is also one-piece, operated by dual hydraulic actuators and features pronounced anhedral. The tailplane is of conventional aluminium skin, rib and stringer construction, as is the tailfin. The ailerons and rudder also employ conventional aluminium alloy skins and ribs, but feature a honeycomb core for lightness and strength. The rudder is non-powered and directional trim is by means of an electrically-driven trim tab. Approximately 30% of the surface of the aircraft is made up of access panels, for ease of maintenance and inspection.

In the event of an ejection, the Hawk's canopy is broken by the miniature detonating cord as the seat is fired. BAe

The Hawk has a low-set one-piece wing and similarly shaped tailplane. BAe/GEOFF LEE

The main undercarriage oleo units are capable of absorbing sink rates in excess of three m/sec. PETER R MARCH

Power for the Hawk T1 is provided by a Rolls-Royce/Turboméca Adour Mk 151 turbofan engine, developing 5,200lb st, which is itself supplied with air from low-set, air intakes. These are positioned ahead of, and slightly above, the wing leading edge providing a measure of protection against foreign object ingestion. The Adour engine is of modular construction for ease of maintenance and repair, and is started using an integral Gas Turbine Starter (GTS). The Adour is renowned for its outstanding reliability and low specific fuel consumption. Engine bleed air is used to provide cockpit pressurisation and conditioning. A shaft, via the gearbox, drives two hydraulic pumps for the dual hydraulic systems. Both systems operate the flying controls but, in addition, the No 1 system also operates general services such as flaps, undercarriage, airbrake and wheel-brakes. The engine also drives a single, brushless 28V generator for DC electrical power, while twin static inverters provide AC electrical power. Two heavy duty batteries, permanently on line with the DC Generator, provide a standby electrical power capability. In the event of

The Hawk's Rolls-Royce/Turboméca Adour Mk 151 has proved reliable and economical. BAe

The Adour turbofan can be removed relatively easily for maintenance or replacement. BAe

total engine failure, or failure of the No 2 hydraulic pump, a Ram Air Turbine (RAT), located in the upper rear fuselage, ahead of the tailfin, extends into the airstream to provide power to the flying controls. Compressed nitrogen accumulators provide emergency lowering of the flaps and undercarriage.

Non-afterburning versions in the Hawk have increased from 5,200lb thrust to 5,845lb for the latest Adour Mk 871 engine. Rolls-Royce, helped by Turboméca, has introduced component improvements throughout the engine to give the operator not only more power but also increased reliability. An increase in low-pressure spool speed, higher-life components, turbine temperature changes and other modifications have given the Adour Mk 871 a 26% thrust improvement over the earlier Mk 861A in high speed, low-level, hot day conditions.

To obtain an engineer's opinion of the Hawk T1, we talked to Chief Technician Terry Riley of No 208(R) Squadron of 4 FTS at RAF Valley. Terry is a highly-experienced crew chief, currently on his second tour of duty with the Hawk and he had this to say about the aircraft:- "It is a good basic aeroplane and that is the key to its success. It is also good basic technology that everybody can understand and work with". Terry then went on to outline the standard maintenance schedule for the aircraft, which involves an on-going programme of inspections and routine maintenance, carried out at 125-hour intervals. As flying hours accumulate, so the inspections become more rigorous until, after 2,000 flying hours, the aircraft is flown to RAF St Athan in Wales, for a complete strip-down inspection and comprehensive programme of maintenance. Every 125 flight hours, the aircraft undergoes a 'Primary' inspection at squadron level, during which the more accessible areas of the structure are examined for signs of damage. The engine and primary systems are also inspected and any necessary maintenance is carried out. The 'Primary' inspection is then followed by a 'Primary Star' inspection every 250 flight hours, a 'Minor' inspection every 500 and a 'Minor Star' inspection every 1,000, leading to the 'Major' inspection at 2,000 flight hours.

Rigid adherence to this programme of inspections and maintenance, has provided timely identification and rectification of potential problems with the Hawk and today enables squadrons, like No 208(R), to generate a high number of operational sorties each working day. In its service career, the Hawk T1 encountered no serious technical fault until the late-1980s, when certain older aircraft that had been used extensively in the punishing, low level, tactical weapons training role. These examples began to experience fatigue cracking in the wings, as predicted from the fatigue test. This led the RAF to initiate, in conjunction with British Aerospace, a fleet-wide wing replacement programme, that will undoubtedly ensure the Hawk continues to provide valuable operational service, well into the 21st Century.

Standard servicing at 125 hour intervals is carried out at the operating base.

Hawks go to RAF St Athan for major servicing after 2,000 flying hours. BRIAN STRICKLAND

THE ROYAL AIR FORCE AEROBATIC TEAM

THE RED ARROWS

Hawks replaced Gnats in 1979. BAe/GEOFF LEE

At least 4,500ft cloud base is needed for this Parasol Break.

Aerobatics have always played a prominent part in Royal Air Force pilot training and allow a new pilot to develop confidence in himself and his aircraft. Formation flying is an essential part of the tactical operations of any front-line squadron. Formation aerobatics not only encourages the growth of confidence in a leader and other members of the formation, but also develops team spirit. The RAF has long recognised the value of display flying in pilot training, as well as for the Service's prestige and for recruiting purposes. Since the earliest days of the Royal Air Force, there have been aerobatic display teams.

The *Red Arrows* was formed in 1965 with seven pilots who gave 65 displays in their HS Gnat trainers that year, winning the Royal Aero Club's Britannia Trophy in recognition of its outstanding contribution in the field of aviation.. The Team expanded to nine pilots in 1968 and since then the classical *Diamond Nine* formation has become their hallmark and is recognised throughout the world as the peak of precision flying. The diminutive HS Gnat was flown by the *Arrows* until the winter of 1979/1980 when it was replaced by the British Aerospace Hawk advanced jet trainer, which the team continues to fly today.

The *Red Arrows* have three basic displays for the public arena. The first is the *Full Display* – consisting of a series of loops, rolls and wing-overs and additionally, full use is made of good weather conditions and wide visibility to demonstrate more exotic set piece manoeuvres. Weather requirements for this display are a cloud base of 4,500ft (1,370m) with a visibility of at least three nautical miles (5km). The second option is the *Rolling Display* – this intermediate show is restricted to rolling aerobatics only and requires a cloud base no lower than 2,500ft (760m). In poor weather conditions (cloud base 1,000ft/305m) the *Flat Display* is flown. This restricted display consists basically of level turns to demonstrate the various formation patterns.

To enable the team to complete more than 100 public displays a year, the *Red Arrows* has a team of 72 engineers and administrators to support its operations. The engineers are divided into two groups: first and second line teams. Twenty-five of the engineers from the first line team provide the specialist support to rectify any minor faults that may occur while the aircraft are operating away from home base. Additionally, three first line engineers are responsible for preparing the aircraft before each flight, which involves refuelling and cleaning the aircraft, checking to ensure that there is no damage to the airframe and engine. Also replenishing the dye and diesel which makes the attractive coloured smoke. The first line engineers travel to most display venues by road, or if a greater distance in a support Hercules. However, nine of the engineers together with the Engineering Officer travel in the back seats of the ten Hawks.

The first line team prepare the Hawks for every display. PETER R MARCH

Today, as international ambassadors for Britain, they are universally acknowledged right around the world, both for their brilliant displays and the qualities of the aircraft they fly, the BAe Hawk. Before the start of the 1995 season the *Red Arrows* had performed no less than 2,906 public displays in 42 different countries and will add a further 100 performances this year, bringing the total to over 3,000.

"Where do the *Red Arrows* go during the winter?" A surprising number of people are under the impression that the *Red Arrows* have little to do in the winter months. Some

A support Hercules carries the team's equipment to overseas venues. PETER R MARCH

The Arrows have been ambassadors for Britain and the BAe Hawk in 42 countries. BAe

people even think the Team disbands at the end of each display season, however nothing could be further from the truth. In many ways the months from October through to April are busier than the display season itself, as the residents of the villages close to RAF Scampton will readily confirm.

Winter is the time for the new pilots to work up. Each year three pilots leave the Team and three new ones join – at least that is the theory. At the end of the 1995 Season only two pilots will leave and so only two new ones will be needed. The following year four pilots will change over. This asymmetry has come about because several years ago a pilot left after only one season; his replacement should have stayed for two years only, but he asked for a full three year tour and was granted his wish. After all, when you have spent your teenage years and early RAF career dreaming of, and working for, a place in the *Red Arrows* it seems churlish to deny that man a full three-year term. So, until someone else leaves early, it seems that the 2 – 4 – 3 sequence will be the norm.

The Team Leader, in conjunction with his pilots, works throughout the winter months choreographing the next season's display. The public expects to see some new manoeuvres every year. The engineers, too, are kept busy

carrying out extensive servicing on the Team's 11 red Hawks so that they should last through the display season, with just the minimum of routine maintenance. Every day throughout the season the engineers have to guarantee that at least 10 of the 11 Hawks are serviceable and available to fly. To ensure that there are sufficient aircraft to meet the daily flying programme during winter, the Team usually borrow two or three Hawks from the Advanced Flying School at RAF Valley. These borrowed aircraft come in a variety of colour schemes and provide regular photo opportunities for the dedicated aircraft spotters.

The Royal Air Force Aerobatic Team (RAFAT) to give the *Red Arrows* its proper title, operates as far as possible like a normal operational squadron. The Team Leader, by rank a squadron leader, is also the Squadron Commander; he is in overall charge of some 80 officers and airmen. The Team Manager, another squadron leader, runs the operational and administration departments. A lot of people think, wrongly, that the Team Manager is the Team Leader; perhaps that is because of the rank – squadron leader – or perhaps it is because the Manager is the one member of the Squadron present on the ground at every single display. In fact there are two other squadron leaders flying as Team members in the 1995 display, but there is only one 'Boss'.

Winter rehearsal, the leader flying a 'borrowed' Hawk from RAF Valley. PETER R MARCH

Take-off. PETER R MARCH

There are three other commissioned officers: two flight lieutenant engineering officers: Eng 1 responsible for the aircraft on the daily flying programme, and Eng 2 for those on hangar maintenance. Finally, there is a full-time public relations officer who is a retired squadron leader pilot.

During the winter months many hundreds of invited visitors come to the *Red Arrows*' Headquarters to see behind the scenes and, they hope, to meet the pilots. These visitors may be captains of industry from businesses that have helped the Team, in one way or another, during the previous season; they may be school children doing projects on flight; Air Training Corps cadets; sick children or sick adults; people celebrating birthdays or wedding anniversaries; or just ordinary members of the public who dote on the *Red Arrows* and want to see them on their own ground. The pilots can never be abrupt with visitors; they must always have a smile on their face, be ready to chat and to answer the same questions they have answered many times before. "How did you become a *Red Arrow*? ". "Why did you want to become a *Red Arrow*? ". "Have you always wanted to be a pilot?"

Winter is also the time for many interviews with newspapers, aviation magazines, and radio and TV stations. Local papers and radio stations need interviews and photo sessions with pilots who hail from their circulation area;

aviation magazines want to hear about the latest new manoeuvres planned; TV stations want up-to-date footage for their libraries. Production teams for television programmes such as *Surprise Surprise, This is Your Life, Jim'll Fix It,* and *How Do They Do That?* descend on RAF Scampton filling up the tiny crew room and briefing room with cameras, lights, cables, microphones and all the other paraphernalia of their profession.

The Winter of 1994/95 was particularly busy. The big topic of conversation was inevitably the forthcoming closure of RAF Scampton, as announced by the Secretary of State for Defence when presenting the Defence Costs' Studies to Parliament. When the closure goes ahead, where will the *Red Arrows* go?

Take one typical day in January 1995 for example:

0740 The duty member of the administrative staff opens up the HQ and switches on the water boiler in the pilots' crew room. That's not all he does, of course, but it is a most important duty. The ground crew have been busy for some time; several aircraft have already been towed out onto the flight line ready for the day's flying. The media, and public, rarely see this early morning activity. Some of the best ground photographs or videos show the immaculately polished red aircraft being towed out of the brightly lit, centrally-heated hangar into the winter gloom.

0750 The PRO is waiting at the Main Guard Room for a photographer and reporter from a well-known Yorkshire newspaper. The reporter is one of the lucky few each year selected for a trip in the back seat of one of the Hawks; the photographer will cover events from the ground. A medical has been booked for 0800hr. Blood pressure, heart, ears and sinuses all have to be examined. His weight, height and leg measurements need to be checked to ensure that they are all within the laid down limits for safe operation of the Martin Baker ejection seat.

Apart from the media, there are dozens of requests each year from members of the public requesting a flight with the *Red Arrows*. The letters are often ingenious, sometimes very touching, but the answer always has to be no. The Hawk is an operational fast jet aircraft not a toy; it is potentially dangerous for unqualified persons and in any case if the Team Leader said 'yes' to one individual request what would he say to all the others?

Once the Medical Officer has declared the reporter fit to fly, he will be issued with all the special flying clothing needed for a flight in a Hawk. The kitting out will take the best part of an hour. After that there will be a detailed briefing with his pilot. He will not be ready before 1100hr at the earliest. Plenty of time for apprehension. "Perhaps I shouldn't have had that fried breakfast after all!"

Close formation. ANDY STEWART

0800 The Synchro Pair, *Reds* 6 and 7, arrive at the Squadron. They are already dressed in most of their flying equipment because they travel to and from their homes on base like that. It saves time. These two are the 'soloists' in the second half of the display. In the early part of the winter they often fly as a pair working out new routines to thrill the crowds. Synchro Leader, *Red 6*, has to check the weather with the Duty Met Officer on the 'phone: the main station briefing is not until 0815hr and that's at the far end of the station. No time for Synchro to go there in person although the Team Leader and Team Manager will usually be at the main briefing with the rest of the Station's pilots. In the meantime Synchro 2, *Red 7*, will be telephoning air traffic control to find out which runway is in use at base and which alternate airfields have been booked. He will be briefed on any air traffic matters that might affect their flight. One of the Synchro Pair will talk on the intercom to the engineers to see which aircraft have been allocated to their flight. During the display season each of the nine display pilots has his own aircraft, with his name painted on the side, but in the winter that is not possible because on any given day several aircraft will be on maintenance in the hangar or away at RAF St Athan for a major overhaul.

Big-T. DANIEL MARCH

0815 The Synchro pilots brief each other. This is a formal briefing but certainly not a formality. Synchro Leader is in charge, even though in 1995 he is a flight lieutenant, while his No 2 is a squadron leader. Synchro Leader has the final say on exactly what the flight profile will be, but it is very much a team effort. Together they review what happened on the previous flight, decide what changes or refinements are needed and go through what they are going to do on the coming flight down to the minutest detail. After signing for the flight on the Authorisation Sheet, the legal document which codifies what they will do during the flight, they zip up their anti-g trousers and go downstairs to Engineering 1st Line Control, where they each collect their flying helmet and check their aircraft's documentation. The Senior NCO in charge briefs them on any pertinent engineering matters, perhaps explaining how any faults reported on the previous flight were rectified.

0825 The pilots walk out to their aircraft parked on the apron a couple of hundred metres away. It is still not fully daylight this January morning. There are some snow covered ice patches around following a recent wintry shower and the wind is quite blustery. The pilots glance up at the sky as they walk, visually checking on the cloud base. Was the Met Man right? Is the lowest cloud really 1600 feet above the airfield? It is difficult to be sure in the half-light.

Distant sounds of shooting, followed by amplified birds' distress calls, indicate that the station's Bird Control Unit is out at work. Actually, it is one man in a yellow Land Rover. He does not shoot the birds; he fires into the air in their vicinity to frighten them off. But Scampton birds are wily birds. The residents know it is only a trick, but they do know to keep out of the way of aircraft. Many of them fly around the airfield at very low level, totally ignoring the mechanical Hawks with their attendant noise and smoke. Unfortunately, every now and again a bird fails to get out of the way. A bird strike is potentially dangerous: it can damage the canopy and hinder the pilot's vision; in the worst case it can cause engine failure.

Out on the flight line the 'see-off' airmen have already completed most of the pilots' pre-flight checks. This is not standard RAF practice, but on *Red Arrows'* Squadron everyone trusts everyone else and it saves the pilots several minutes at the start of every flight. The airmen greet the pilots and help them strap into the ejection seats. Within seconds the pilots are ready, canopies close and the pilots are snugly sealed into their pressurised offices.

A point of procedure, that not many of the public know about, concerns the movement of the aircraft canopies. The

Roll-back. PETER R MARCH

airman standing at the nose of the aircraft always turns his back on the pilot when the canopy is opened or closed. This is for safety reasons. There is just a remote possibility that as the canopy moves up or down the miniature detonating cord (MDC) embedded in the perspex could fire. The MDC is designed to fire the instant a pilot operates his ejection seat handle; the canopy shatters and the seat has a clear passage out of the aircraft. If the perspex shatters on the ground, sharp pieces fly off in all directions and could cause serious injury to any unprotected person in the vicinity. The system is, however, very reliable and the only occasion in recent years when the MDC has been fired inadvertently was, it has to be said, the fault of the pilot sitting in the aircraft.

Thumbs up from the groundcrew, the igniters tick rhythmically and the engines roar into life. Synchro Leader calls Air Traffic Control for taxi clearance. Runway 05 is in use, that is the north-easterly runway, heading out over the A15 Ermine Street towards the former Lightning base at RAF Binbrook. There will be a strong crosswind component from the right on take-off.

0833 A Hercules transport aircraft, arriving empty from its base at RAF Lyneham in Wiltshire to pick up a Scampton-based British arms control team bound for Kiev, lands. Fat Albert, a soubriquet for the aircraft – not the pilot, has to clear the runway before 0840, Synchro's scheduled take-off time. "Lights at three miles", reports the Hercules captain to Air Traffic Control. That means the cloud base is OK for Synchro, but the visibility is not too good. When the Synchro pair are flying directly towards each other for their opposition manoeuvres, they have a closing speed of 12 miles per minute, that is one mile in just five seconds.

The pilots wave the chocks away and Synchro are on the move, taxiing past the four pre-World War 2 hangars, past the grave of *Nigger*, Wing Commander Guy Gibson VC's dog that was killed on the main road outside RAF Scampton on the night of No 617 Squadron's The 'Dams' raid, past Foxtrot Dispersal in the south-eastern corner of the airfield where other ground crew are waiting to receive

Above and below: *Synchro action.* PETER R MARCH

the Hercules, and eventually turning right onto the 9,000ft runway, that was especially built in the mid-fifties for the RAF's V Force.

0840 The Synchro Pair take off in close formation. This is the start of Slot 1. There are six half-hour slots every day reserved for the *Red Arrows*. During each of those periods no other aircraft, military or civilian, is allowed inside a cylindrical section of airspace known as Restricted Area 313. R313 is five nautical miles in radius, centred on the Scampton Air Traffic Control tower and extends from ground level to 9,500 ft above the ground. Synchro usually fly the early slot: "It gives the rest of the pilots an extra half hour in bed!" There is no surveillance radar at Scampton these days but there is at RAF Waddington, just a few miles away on the other side of Lincoln. The controllers there will keep a very close eye on R313 for the next half hour and remind any transitting aircraft of the need to stay well clear.

0900 The other *Red Arrows*' pilots have arrived at the Squadron in the last 30 minutes, one of them with just seconds to spare. Also present is a flight lieutenant from another station who has applied to join the *Red Arrows* at the end of the 1995 season. He will fly with the Leader today to get a first hand impression of what the job is like. There will be many more like him in the following weeks. The

newspaper photographer and reporter have just arrived with the PRO from Sick Quarters; the reporter has passed his medical and the adrenalin is beginning to flow. At exactly 0900 one of the pilots rings the bell on the wall, the signal for the met briefing to start. Everyone congregates around the coffee bar to listen to the Met Man, but they glance surreptitiously out of the windows every now and again as the Synchro pair roar past.

The winter weather at Scampton is rarely straightforward. The airfield perches on the edge of the Lincoln Cliff, with no higher ground to the east until the Urals. Today, apparently, the low stratus may or may not clear; the bitterly cold cross wind may, or may not, go out of limits; runway braking action was reported as good by the Hercules pilot, but there were icy patches in places – watch out in case of an aborted take-off! The air temperature is plus one but the wind creates a chill factor of minus 10. One of the pilots needs to know yesterday's high temperature at RAF Akrotiri in Cyprus. He keeps a chart going which compares the Scampton temperature with that at Akrotiri. The Team deploys to Cyprus every April for final rehearsals in guaranteed good weather and without many of the distractions they get at Scampton. It cheers everyone up to learn how much warmer it is in Cyprus than at Scampton, although for one week in March 1994 it was actually warmer at Scampton than in Akrotiri.

0905 The PRO introduces the pressmen and reminds everyone that an important group of 'upstairs' visitors is expected at 1140. The term 'upstairs' is used to differentiate between those visitors who meet the pilots in the crew room and have a buffet lunch with them, from the masses of ordinary visitors who do not go upstairs into the inner

The team's final rehearsals are conducted in Cyprus. ANDY STEWART

sanctum. If the pilots had to meet and chat to every visitor they would never get any work done. Eng 1 (the First Line Engineering Officer) reports that there will be seven serviceable aircraft for slot 2. "OK", says the Boss calling his bluff, "We'll fly the front seven in slot 2. Brief at 25." The Boss then takes a coffee along to his office where he spends a few minutes looking through his paper-work. The admin corporal has already sorted the contents of the Squadron Commander's in-tray so that the most important papers are at the top and the 'niff-naff' lower down. The corporal has to be adept at sorting the wheat from the chaff.

0910 The reporter barely has time to finish his coffee before he is whisked off downstairs to the Flying Clothing section where he will be kitted out with everything from thermal underwear and socks, to flying boots and helmet and everything in-between. It is important to wear non-flammable clothing next to the skin in case of a fiery accident and in winter it is most important to wear a number of layers of clothing to protect against hypothermia whilst waiting for rescue, in the event of an ejection over wild country. The photographer hangs around watching and taking photographs, although some will not be suitable for publication – not in a daily newspaper anyway.

0925 Exactly on the dot, the pre-flight briefing for slot 2 starts. Accurate timing is provided by a radio controlled wall clock that is synchronised with a time signal transmitted from Rugby, the clock a gift to the Team from a well-known watch manufacturer. One of the pilots has some private guests who sit in the back row listening intently as the Boss briefs the sortie, although to them it sounds like a different language. The briefing is short and to the point – it has to be because take-off is scheduled for 0955. The Synchro pilots pass through the briefing room on their way in and give the Team Leader a weather report. Those two grab a coffee and then take over the briefing room for their debrief of Slot 1. They will fly again in Slot 3, take off at 1110, but before then they have to try and find time to give a short interview to the newspaper reporter.

Crossover. DANIEL MARCH

0955 "*Reds* rolling go!" Exactly on time to the nearest second the brakes are released and the seven red aircraft accelerate along the runway. In the meantime the newspaper reporter has finished his kitting out. He feels very conspicuous clumping awkwardly around in heavy leather boots and g-suit, the elasticised garment which fits tightly around the waist and lower limbs. When the aircraft accelerates against the force of gravity, high pressure air from the engine's compressor is forced into the g-suit: the more the g, the greater the pressure. This has the effect of squeezing the arteries in the lower abdomen and legs, thereby preventing all the blood rushing down to the toes. On this flight he will experience at least 4g, when every part of his body, internal and external, will weigh four times normal. You cannot accurately describe this to someone: it has to be experienced. The *Red Arrows* pull up to 7g in their display, Synchro Pair sometimes more than that.

1000 While the seven are airborne the PRO settles the photographer and reporter down in front of a TV set to watch a passenger video brief about the ejection seat and emergency drills. The film lasts 15 minutes and has to be seen by every passenger who flies in the back seat of a Hawk. It is very comprehensive: it aims to cover every possible eventuality and, because of that, it can be alarming to a nervous passenger. As the video finishes the Manager, callsign *Red 10*, comes in to brief the reporter about his forthcoming sortie. This allows the PRO to go back to his office and start dealing with the morning mail and the many calls that will have been stored on his answerphone by this time.

1030 The seven have landed from Slot 2, taxied in to dispersal, closed down and reported any snags to the ground crew. Then they go upstairs to their crew room for a cup of coffee and a biscuit. In the meantime the *Red Arrows* video man, who has been filming Slot 2 from a spot in front of Air Traffic Control, places the video cassette in the machine in the briefing room. The bell rings again and the pilots settle down for debriefing. The Leader gives his first thoughts about the sortie and then runs the video, stopping frequently to freeze-frame the picture and study in detail exactly who was out of position and why. There can be no argument: the video-camera never lies. The debriefing can last up to an hour in the early part of the training season; it is rarely less than 30 minutes even at the end of the display season. Every single practice sortie and every single public display is recorded on video and debriefed in this way. Only when the Leader is sure that every lesson, that can be learnt, has been learnt does the debriefing end.

1050 *Red 10* and his passenger walk out to the flight line and pose for the obligatory picture by the nose of the aircraft. It takes about 10 minutes to get the reporter properly strapped in; in spite of his pre-flight coaching, he is all fingers and thumbs, but that is quite normal. When the pilot is satisfied that his passenger is happy, he climbs into the front seat and quickly straps himself in. Once a passenger is strapped in it is best to get moving as quickly as possible. In any case they must be airborne before 1110, which is when Synchro are due to take off in Slot 3. No delays. Fifteen minutes later they are airborne and clearing

Debriefing using the video film of the practice is an essential part of every training flight. PETER R MARCH

off out of the circuit to fly northwards to Yorkshire to have a look at the reporter's local area. The Hercules, having completed embarkation of the arms control inspectors and their accoutrements, takes off just in front of Synchro and sets course for the Ukraine.

1105 In the meantime the day's 'upstairs' visitors have checked in at the Main Guard Room and been met by the PRO. They are nine senior executives from a well-known company that has provided the Team with a lot of support behind the scenes during the previous season. The Ministry of Defence does not allow companies to use their connection with the *Red Arrows* for overt advertising purposes. The visitors are taken to a small museum-cum-briefing room in the Central Flying School (CFS) HQ, at the far end of the airfield from the *Red Arrows*' hangar. There they are given a short slide presentation about the history of RAF Scampton, CFS and the *Red Arrows*. There are two reasons for going to CFS to do this: one, to keep the visitors away from the pilots while they are still debriefing slot 2; two, the CFS is an interesting place in its own right. CFS is the oldest flying school in the world having been continuously in service since 1912 when a Royal Navy captain became the first Commandant, appointed by no less a person than Winston Churchill, who was at that time First Sea Lord. The *Red Arrows* have been an integral part of CFS from the earliest days when all Team members were qualified flying instructors.

1110 The Synchro Pair are airborne again on their second sortie of the day – Slot 3. The reporter, perhaps without realising it, has missed his opportunity for an interview; he and *Red 10* are heading, at 400 mph, for the Humber Bridge and 'God's Own County'.

1140 The upstairs visitors, accompanied by the PRO, arrive at the *Red Arrows*' HQ just in time to see Synchro Pair taxi back into dispersal. The other pilots have finished their debrief and are ready to welcome their guests. There are only a few minutes for socialising because the time is rapidly approaching for Slot 4. Seven aircraft will fly again. The engineers are doing a good job keeping nine aircraft out of nine serviceable; each aircraft has already flown two sorties and the day is not half over.

1155 Once more the bell rings. The visiting pilot will be flying a second sortie with the Team Leader. In addition, the Commandant of CFS, an air commodore, will be flying with *Red 4*, one of the new pilots for 1995, to see how he is getting on. With overall responsibility for the *Red Arrows*, the Commandant regularly flies with the Team and, just as regularly, watches their progress from the ground. This time the upstairs visitors are occupying the back two rows of seats in the briefing room. Just outside they can see a single Hawk taxying back onto the apron: that is *Red 10* and the reporter returning from their foray into Yorkshire. A few flakes of snow are blowing around in the easterly wind – the Met man was right about that.

The visitors, huddled into warm top coats, watch Slot 4 from the prime position, 'Display Datum', directly in front of Air Traffic Control alongside the video man. The whole display is centred on Display Datum as the name implies. Datum represents the VIP enclosure at a public display. Datum is where the Synchro Pair aim to cross in front of each other. Datum is where the Manager usually stands to give his public commentary. Datum is very cold today. "How long do they fly for?" someone asks plaintively. Never mind him. . . Datum is the place to be!

1300 Everyone, including the Synchro Pair, is back in the crew room by 1300hr. The visitors help themselves from a light finger buffet with still half-frozen fingers. The PRO is there with the photographer who is taking fly-on-the-wall pictures. The reporter, having changed back into civilian clothes, joins in with everyone else; he is a much braver man now that the sortie is over. To his intense relief he was not airsick. There will be much to tell his colleagues back in the news room.

The visitors are invited to sit in on the debrief. They don't understand everything that is said, but at least they can watch the video and marvel at how finicky the pilots are about each other's performances. "I told you he was out of position", whispers one visitor knowingly to his colleague. It is only a practice of course.

1400 The photographer is anxious to get back to his office and develop his films and the reporter has to let the sub-editor loose on the words. They hope to print the story tomorrow. They promise to send the PRO a copy of the paper; the *Red Arrows* always like to read about themselves – as long as the reporter has got all his facts right!

1425 The slot 4 debriefing has barely ended but it is already time for another pre-flight briefing. Synchro Pair did not fly in Slot 5 at 1340 because of the passing snow shower. The weather has now improved and the Team Leader has decided to fly slot 6, take off at 1455. All nine aircraft remain serviceable but this time the Synchro Pair

Servicing continues on the Red Arrow's *Hawks throughout the winter, to prepare them for a rigorous new season.* PETER R MARCH

The team flies with other aircraft, like this British Airways Concorde, on special occasions. PETER R MARCH

will fly in their accustomed positions as *Reds 6* and *7* directly behind the Leader. *Reds 3* and *5* will stay on the ground so there are spare aircraft in case one goes unserviceable on start up. The resulting seven-aircraft formation, the right hand side of a *Diamond Nine*, looks a bit lop-sided but is good practice, in particular for two of the new pilots, *Reds 2* and *4*. The upstairs visitors have gone into the hangar to take a close look at the aircraft undergoing major servicing and to drop in on the *Red Arrows* souvenir shop.

1455 Seven aircraft airborne again. The spares were not required so the ground crew tow them back into the hangar. The upstairs visitors were expected to depart at 1500 but, when invited, could not resist the temptation to watch Slot 6. This time they watch from in front of the Team's HQ and get a quite different view.

1530 The last formation sortie for the day is over. As the pilots walk back to the crew room from their aircraft they pause on the grass to chat to a group of visiting children and sign autographs. They cannot afford to stay outdoors long because they are hot and sweaty from the cockpit and it is bitterly cold talking to the children. The last thing any pilot needs is a head cold which would prevent him from flying. The visiting children will have a close look at one of the

Hawks in the hangar; one or two of them may be allowed to sit in a cockpit and have photographs taken. All the other visitors have left. As the final pilot debriefing for the day starts, the ground crew begin towing the aircraft back into the hangar. Already the sky is darkening. The temperature, which had struggled up to a maximum of two degrees just after midday, is again hovering on zero and more snow is forecast.

Marking the retirement of the last RAF Vulcan over Cranfield in September 1992. PETER R MARCH

A single Hawk remains out on the flight line; one of the pilots has to fly down to Exeter to give an evening lecture to a local aviation society. It will be a night landing at Exeter Airport, but that should not be a problem as the weather is much better in the south west. The pilot will stay overnight before returning early the following day, weather permitting, in time to fly slot 2 with the rest of the Team.

Now it is time for the Team Leader's weekly meeting with the Manager and PRO to discuss the following week's PR events and schedule of visitors. There will be upstairs visitors every single day. Additionally, an independent TV company is due to be with the Team for two days making a seven minute item for a new BBC series. Two days' work for a seven minute item is about par for television, but the Director has still not decided exactly which shots he wants to include. It is not easy to convince him that *Red Arrows'* time is just as valuable as his. The meeting goes on until 1730 when the Boss and the Manager go to their own offices to start dealing with the day's accumulated business.

240 air nautical miles to the south west, *Red 9* is just landing at Exeter airport; his day is not yet over. By this time most of the other pilots have either gone home or adjourned to their 'quiet' room to get on with fan mail and secondary duties.

A unique formation at Bratislava in September 1992 – Red Leader with a White Albatros L-39 Albatros, Patrouille de France Alpha Jet, Frecce Tricolori MB339, Patrulla Aguila Aviojet and Russian Test Pilots' Sukhoi Su-27. PETER R MARCH

The last person to leave the *Red Arrows'* HQ is the admin clerk who locks up at 1815. The end of another typical winter day for the *Red Arrows*.

.....But not quite. The engineers are still working in the hangar. They do not finish until enough aircraft are serviceable for the following day's flying programme

Squadron Leader Tony Cunnane

Red Arrows *in the Middle East accompanied by two support Hercules.* BAe

At the end of the day, the RAF Red Arrows and the BAe Hawk have made a tremendous contribution as aerial ambassadors for the Service and the aviation industry at home and abroad. BAe

GOSHAWK

The first T-45A (162787) on its maiden flight on 16 April 1988, with DAC test pilot Fred Hamilton at the controls. BAe/MDC

The T-45A Goshawk was developed from the Hawk, as part of a new training system for the US Navy. The process began in 1975, when the US Naval Air Development Center examined the feasibility of replacing the T-2C Buckeye and TA-4J Skyhawk with a single aircraft and new training system that would carry out both the intermediate and advanced phases of the undergraduate flight training process. The programme, known as VTX-TS, covered a total training system, which included the academic syllabus and ground based simulators. Contractor maintenance with Integrated Logistics Support was required, whereby the US Navy would contract out all aircraft maintenance tasks.

It was perceived, within British Aerospace, that with suitable modifications to allow aircraft carrier operations, the Hawk had the potential to be an effective naval trainer. BAe gave a presentation on the Hawk to US Navy representatives in May 1978, and subsequent studies confirmed the feasibility of the necessary modifications. A teaming agreement with McDonnell Douglas followed in January 1980, and the two companies then entered a period of intense competition with several other contenders. These included Dassault-Breguet and Dornier teamed with Lockheed, proposing a modified Alpha Jet, and Aermacchi teamed with Advanced Technology Systems in promoting the MB339. In addition, projects indigenous to the USA included proposals from Grumman, General Dynamics, Northrop, Rockwell and a new design from Douglas Aircraft, identified as the D-7000.

The US Navy announced its selection of a Hawk derivative on 19 November 1981, with the Douglas Aircraft Company (DAC) as prime contractor, British Aerospace (BAe) as principal subcontractor for the airframe, Rolls-Royce for the engine and Sperry (subsequently Honeywell and now Hughes) for simulators. Definition of the contract for full scale development of the aircraft took several years, with the contract award achieved in October 1984.

Minimum development cost was a prime requirement and this factor was a major driver in the choice of a derivative aircraft. The US Navy directed that the T-45 Training System programme was to be run as an 'austere', minimum cost programme. A 1984 'Tiger Team' review resulted in almost a 50% reduction in the planned development cost.

Construction of two prototypes began in February 1986. The first T-45A, BuNo 162787, took to the air on 16 April 1988 at Long Beach, California, with DAC test pilot Fred Hamilton at the controls. The aircraft was ferried to the DAC Flight Test Center at Yuma, Arizona later the same month. The second aircraft, BuNo 162788, was flown to Yuma by test pilot Gary Smith on 2 November 1988, on its first flight.

A stronger undercarriage with twin nosewheels, revised forward fuselage shape, full-span flap vane and arrester hook clearly differentiate the T-45A from the Hawk T1. BAe/MDC

The T-45 designation includes the 'A' suffix as a result of an initial US Navy plan to take delivery of 54 solely land based T-45Bs, in order to achieve an earlier in-service date for the new aircraft. The US Navy dropped this plan in 1984 when it decided to concentrate the production order in favour of the T-45A.

There are a number of significant differences between the Hawk and the T-45A design. The T-45A has a stronger landing gear, with twin nose wheels, launch catapult bar and hold back. The main wheels are located further outboard, and the necessary arrester hook is carried on the rear fuselage.

The fuselage structure was modified to absorb the catapult and arrestment loads, modifications to the wing to increase strength included completely new wing skins and a new major forging for rib 7, which mounts the main landing gear. The new structural changes were incorporated to give the aircraft a 14,400 hour fatigue life, on the basis of a structural design factor of 2 and fatigue testing for two lifetimes, allowing an operational life of 20 years based on a planned US Navy usage of 720 hours per year.

The Hawk's under fuselage air brake was replaced by twin side-mounted speed brakes to accommodate the arrester hook, and to allow use of the speed brakes throughout the

approach and landing to provide additional drag. A low speed yaw damper was installed to improve directional stability in the approach configuration, and the wing dressing was modified to cater for the higher lift

Rear view showing the T-45A's side-mounted speed brakes and arrester hook. MDC

Improvements included a small horizontal fin (or 'smurf') forward of the stabilator, wing leading edge slat and larger tail feathers.

D M STROUD COLLECTION

requirements of the T-45A. This included the re-introduction of the original Hawk full span flap vane, although it resulted in a tendency for tailplane stall when flying with full flap and the landing gear up. A small horizontal fin was added forward of the stabilator to eliminate a this tailplane stall tendency.

The T-45 was equipped with the Rolls-Royce Turboméca Adour Mk 861 engine, as installed in the Hawk Mk 60 series, but derated to Mk 851 thrust levels to give increased engine life. The Adour for the T-45A, known as the F405-RR-400, also incorporated a mechanical fuel system as a back up to the electronic engine control amplifier.

The modifications to the Hawk design baseline were limited by the need for minimum cost in accordance with the US Navy's austere programme philosophy. The results of Navy evaluations of the T-45, however, led to later demands for further modifications in order to meet operational requirements. Ultimately, the aircraft was fitted with a wing leading edge slat, larger tail feathers, an improved yaw damper and rudder lock mechanism, aileron/rudder interconnection and an improved speed brake system. In addition, a higher thrust Adour engine with improved throttle response was installed. The result of these changes was an increase in the aircraft's empty weight,

from the 7,940lb of the basic 50-series Hawk to 9,860lb for the T-45A. Although externally very similar to the Hawk the T-45A is a very different aircraft.

The application of the minimum development cost philosophy had a profound effect on the planned flight testing. The 1984 'Tiger Team' review resulted in a severe reduction in the scope of the flight test programme. The most significant element of the review was that a large proportion of the planned test flying hours were eliminated and the number of test aircraft was reduced from four to two, on the basis that the T-45 was to be a minimum change from the Hawk. Maximum use was to be made of existing Hawk Flight Test Data, in order to minimise the number of flying hours required.

Flight testing of the T-45 started in earnest in late June 1988, after the installation of the necessary instrumentation had been completed on BuNo 162787 in Yuma. The early testing covered flight envelope expansion, general handling characteristics and performance, low-speed handling and initial carrier suitability work. The results of the first few test flights were encouraging. The aircraft was found to be agile and tightly controlled, like the Hawk; control forces were light, but not objectionably so, and all the pilots who flew the aircraft praised its handling characteristics at mid-range speeds in the cruise configuration. Many pilots were also favourably surprised by its low fuel consumption.

A number of problems were, however, encountered early in the demonstration programme. It became evident, as the programme progressed, that some effort would be required to improve stall performance and low speed lateral and directional flying characteristics. Operation of the side mounted speed brake resulted in a pitch change which, although within the limits of the specification, was determined to be undesirable and simulated carrier approach tests showed that an increase in engine thrust was needed for hot weather operations, with landing gear and flaps down. During the envelope expansion tests, a divergent longitudinal control oscillation was encountered at 475kt, which resulted from a coupling between the dynamic characteristic of the aircraft and its control system. A temporary restriction to the flight envelope limiting maximum speed to 340kt was imposed until a modification to the longitudinal control system was incorporated early in 1989.

The Yuma tests were concluded with a US Navy Development and Operational Test (DT/OT) held at the end of 1988, shortly after the second test aircraft joined the programme. Immediately following completion of the US Navy evaluations, the two test aircraft and the test team

The first T-45A was used extensively in the flight test development programme until it was destroyed in a landing accident in June 1992. MDC

relocated to the Naval Air Test Center (NATC) at Patuxent River in Maryland, where the remainder of the test programme was to be accomplished.

The US Navy evaluation had been deliberately conducted at that stage in the programme, in order to obtain early customer comments. The evaluators report on this initial evaluation stated that the T-45A was considered to possess limited potential for success in the training mission, and included a long list of alleged deficiencies. The DT/OT

For the latter part of 1990, four T-45As were involved in the test programme. MDC

report heralded the beginning of a difficult year for the T-45 programme. Most of the alleged deficiencies identified by the Navy test team were relatively minor items, but several required resolution before the aircraft could be cleared by the US Navy for service use. The most serious of these covered stall performance, engine thrust and throttle response, the pitch change associated with speed brake operation, unsatisfactory lateral and directional stability, and the need for modification of the longitudinal control system. These became known as the 'Big Five', and the test programme at NATC initially concentrated on evaluating solutions to these apparent problems.

The longitudinal control system was modified by the inclusion of viscous dampers and changes to the balance of some control rods. This satisfactorily eliminated the coupled oscillation and allowed the flight envelope to be opened up. Modifications to the speed brake included enlarging the actuator and strengthening the attachment structure. This allowed an increase in speed brake deflection at high speed, thus improving its effectiveness. The incorporation of an interconnect between the speed brake and the tailplane reduced pitch changes, resulting from speed brake deployment.

Lateral and directional characteristics were improved through the use of an extended ventral fin and an improved yaw damper. In addition, an interconnection between the rudder and ailerons was introduced to eliminate an adverse yaw present at low speeds. Engine thrust was improved in stages, initially by restoring the thrust to Adour Mk 861 levels, and eventually by the selection of the 5,845lb thrust Adour Mk 871, known as the F405-RR-401. Throttle response was improved through changes to the engine fuel control unit and engine electronic control amplifier.

Efforts to improve stall performance and characteristics constituted a large portion of the flight test programme conducted during 1989. The requirement was to demonstrate a lift coefficient large enough to allow an approach speed of no more than 125kt true air speed (TAS) at an aircraft weight of 11,600lb, while retaining stall characteristics acceptable to the US Navy. This objective was finally achieved in late summer 1989, but by then the US Navy had decided, through the Navy chartered

T-45A Goshawk No 1 (162787) making its first carrier landing on the USS John F Kennedy *on 4 December 1991.* MDC

Configuration Action Team (CAT), that additional lift would be required to allow for planned future weight growth.

The CAT was the culmination of the US Navy's efforts to direct Douglas to make improvements to the T-45. Early in 1989, the US Navy had established an Independent Assessment Team (IAT), consisting of experienced service and industry personnel not connected with the T-45 programme. The purpose of the assessment was to determine whether the T-45A could be improved to meet the Navy's operational desires. The recommendations of the IAT were not to be constrained by the requirements of the aircraft specification. The IAT concluded that modifications to the T-45 would enable the aircraft to meet the Navy's operational goals, and following completion of the IAT studies, the CAT was established.

The purpose of the CAT, which consisted of representatives of the US Navy and the contractors, was to determine which of the IAT's recommendations should be embodied. The result of the team activity was that the Navy directed McDonnell Douglas (given full responsibility for

the T-45TS programme at St Louis from 19 December 1989) to incorporate a number of modifications to the T-45. The most significant and far reaching of these modifications was the introduction of a wing leading edge slat, to be extended as the flaps extended. The slatted wing was to be designed to produce a lift coefficient high enough to meet the specified approach speed, while providing the

Above: *The first T-45A on board the USS* John F Kennedy. MDC

Navy with a margin of lift to allow for future weight growth. The design of the slatted wing was started by a joint McDonnell Douglas/BAe team in the autumn of 1989, and the first production wing incorporating a slat was delivered to St Louis in the summer of 1991. In order to minimise any delays to the test programme, a wing fitted with a fixed retracted slat was installed on BuNo 162788 in the summer of 1990, and a fixed extended slat was flown on BuNo 162787 in the autumn of 1990. This period also saw the introduction of two further test aircraft. BuNo 163599 was intended to be the first production aircraft, but in order to reduce the delays then being experienced, the decision was taken to install test instrumentation and include it in the test programme. It was fitted with a wing incorporating a fixed retracted slat. The fourth Goshawk (BuNo 163600) was used for maintenance manual validation.

Flight testing continued through to the end of 1990, when a further formal evaluation by the US Navy test team was accomplished. The result was a statement from the Navy that the aircraft now exhibited satisfactory potential for the jet training mission. This effectively gave the green light for the remainder of the flight test programme, and the flight envelope was expanded in stages to 550kt and Mach 1.04. The normal acceleration envelope was expanded to the design limit for the aircraft of -4g to +7.33g. The handling characteristics of the aircraft during flight at high angle of attack were investigated, and initial spin testing was accomplished. Further work outstanding at the beginning of 1991 included stores carriage and release, and the majority of the carrier suitability work. Work-up for the initial sea trials began in the summer of 1991, and the T-45 made its first deck landing on the USS *John F Kennedy* on 4 December 1991, some 3½ years after its first flight. The aircraft carrier trials were very successful, with no major difficulties being encountered.

The problems were not yet over, however, and the discovery of unexpected spin modes on the aircraft led to a need for more detailed testing. The flight loads measurement tests accomplished during 1991 revealed some unexpected problems with the original design loads, and this resulted in the need for additional structural modifications. The test programme was further impacted as a result of a landing accident involving BuNo 162787 at Edwards Air Force Base in June 1992. The pilot ejected safely from the aircraft following a loss of directional control after landing, and the aircraft was written off in the subsequent departure from the runway. The effect of the loss of this valuable test aircraft was a significant delay to the test programme.

The culmination of the T-45A Full Scale Development Programme occurred at the end of 1993 when the formal US Navy Technical Evaluation (TECHEVAL) was accomplished. This was followed in early 1994 by the US Navy Operational Evaluation (OPEVAL). The T-45 aircraft and training system passed the evaluations with flying colours, the OPEVAL report stating that 'the T-45TS is determined to be operationally effective for ground school, familiarisation, basic instruments, radio instruments, airways navigation, instrument rating, formation and night familiarisation training'.

The story of the T-45 development has not yet ended, although the US Navy has concluded that the Goshawk (so named to avoid clashing with the 'Hawk' missile) is satisfactory for its needs, and much future development seems unlikely in the current restricted funding environment. The original proposals for the T-45 included a modern digital 'glass' cockpit, similar to that installed in the F/A-18 Hornet, but US Navy funding constraints led to its deletion, and the first T-45 aircraft flew with conventional cockpit instrumentation. The decision to delete the 'glass' cockpit was later reviewed by the Navy, and a full digital cockpit is now proposed for introduction into

The full digital 'Cockpit 21' is planned for introduction on the production line in 1997. MDC

The first Goshawk assembled at St Louis (163601) was flown on 16 December 1991. MDC

The handing over ceremony of the first Goshawk for the US Navy (163601) took place at St Louis on 23 January 1992. MDC

the aircraft. Flight development of the system, known as 'Cockpit 21' started in March 1994. Although the cost cutters' axe is presently poised, the system is planned to go into line build production with first deliveries scheduled for early 1997.

The development programme also included ground testing, which continued in parallel with the flight development activity. The ground test work including static and drop tests, was undertaken by McDonnell Douglas, the fatigue test by BAe at Brough, hydraulic tests at Kingston and wind tunnel tests at Weybridge, Warton and Farnborough. The static and drop tests have been successfully completed, including a drop test at a vertical velocity of 28 feet per second. The fatigue test programme, however, was delayed by the US Navy requirements for the installation of the slatted wing and test rig modifications resulting from increased loads. At the time of writing, work is in progress at BAe Brough, with one half lifetime of

testing complete, and is expected to reach one full lifetime of testing by early 1996.

The teaming agreement between BAe and McDonnell Douglas specified how the design, test and manufacture work was to be shared between the companies. Final assembly and manufacture of the forward fuselage was to be undertaken by the Douglas Aircraft Company, although BAe retained a large manufacturing work share, with the responsibility for production of the wings, empennage and rear fuselage. T-45 manufacture was to be located initially at Long Beach, with the production line later moving to Palmdale, California. In late 1989, however, McDonnell Douglas decided to move the entire T-45 programme from Long Beach to St Louis, Missouri. The transfer of work was completed by the end of 1990, and the first T-45 built in St Louis, the third production Goshawk (163601), was flown on 16 December 1991.

Production of the T-45 continued throughout the

The first student class completed its course wtih carrier operations in the summer of 1994. MDC

development programme, with the exception of delay resulting from the slatted wing modification, and by the end of 1994 a total of 48 production aircraft had been delivered to the US Navy at NAS Kingsville, Texas. Of these, two (163629 and 163639) were lost in a mid-air collision which claimed the life of one student pilot, and one (163635) is presently based at St Louis for flight development of the glass cockpit. Several of the aircraft were complete before all the modifications introduced after the first DT/OT were installed, and there is a modification programme in place at Kingsville, run by McDonnell Douglas, to bring all aircraft up to the agreed modification standard. At any one time, four aircraft are undergoing modification. The reliability of the aircraft has been found to be excellent, and the US Navy flying rates are in excess of the 60 hours per month original requirement. Instructor training started in 1992, and the first student class to gain its wings on the T-45A graduated in September 1994.

The US Defense Acquisition Board finally gave the go ahead for full rate production of the T-45A in January 1995, although it is not expected that the production rate will exceed the current 12 aircraft per year. Defense budget cutbacks have reduced the Navy's current Goshawk requirement from the originally planned 300 aircraft to 174, and plans to operate the T-45A from NAS Meridian (TW1/VT-7) are likely to be abandoned, as Meridian is on the current list of bases scheduled to be closed.

The development of the T-45A has been an interesting and challenging chapter in the history of the Hawk. The programme has shown that a good land-based aircraft can be successfully modified to introduce a capability for carrier operations. Although the current drive is for continued reduction in costs, there can be no doubt that the US Navy now has an extremely capable, safe and cost effective training system which will provide for its needs well into the next century.

Instructor training commenced in 1992 and included extensive flying from the USS Forrestal. MDC

Texas day-break. Goshawks on Training Wing 2's flight line at NAS Kingsville. MDC

TRAINERS FOR THE WORLD

During the long days of Finland's short summer, training sorties can continue almost round the clock. PETER HOLMAN

FINLAND

Even at 11 o'clock at night, as the two pilots strap into their ejector seats and start pre-flight cockpit checks, the sun is not far below the horizon. Its subdued light fills the western sky and the ground crew busy themselves around the green-camouflaged Hawk without need of torches as the student pilot in the front seat closes the canopy.

The Adour engine hums into life, brakes are released and the Hawk trundles smartly along the tree-lined taxiway to the fighter base's main runway. Within seconds, the jet is climbing towards the west, silhouetted clearly against a light evening sky that is stubbornly refusing to darken. By midnight, when the Hawk returns, a dull twilight fills the sky, still providing enough visibility for the pilot clearly to identify terrain features on his approach to base.

This is literally the lighter side of a student fighter-pilot's life in the Finnish Air Force, where during the almost never-ending days of the short summer he can fly sortie after sortie with few interruptions, such as darkness and bad weather. Neither intervenes much during June and July, the two months when the Finns and their Air Force are spared the challenges of their cold, dark winters.

"This is a time of year when utilisation of the Hawks is particularly high", explains Major Mikko Sovelius, a senior pilot of the Finnish Air Force's Satakunta Wing at Pirkkala air force base near Tampere in central southern Finland. Major Sovelius and the instructors and students in his charge appreciate the Hawk's reliability and its flexibility as a modern multi-role training machine, for Satakunta Wing's role is to defend central and south-western Finland on a 24-hour-a-day, all-year-round basis. The short summer months are packed with flying training.

"Our new pilots have already completed 90 hours' basic flying training on the L-70 Vinka piston-engined trainer, followed by 30 hours on our Hawk simulator and another 110 hours, at least, advanced training on Hawks at our air academy", explains Major Sovelius. "Then they are posted to one of the Air Force's three main wings".

"For those who come here, we provide a further 100 hours on the Hawk to turn them from *competent* Hawk pilots into *expert* Hawk pilots, who also know how to fight in the air". This conversion involves air-to-ground and air-to-air gunnery, one-to-one dogfights, radar-directed combat tactics and long-range patrols. The successful pilot

A Hawk flying over Finland's desolate tundra on a busy mid-summer training flight. BAe

then graduates to two-seat versions of the Finnish Air Force's supersonic interceptors, the Swedish-built Saab Draken or the Soviet-built MiG-21.

For the young Hawk pilots and their aircraft this 100 hours represents much hard flying, not just in the blossom-scented summer air but mostly in the arctic and sub-arctic weather of Finland's winter climate. Ground temperatures below -40°, heavy cloud cover, frequent icing conditions and frosty fogs are common challenges for Finnish Air Force pilots. Throughout winter, daylight hours are few and sometimes (such as in Lapland) virtually non-existent. The geography of the country, too, is a challenge. Nearly 70% of Finland is forest, another 10% lakes and the remainder mostly farms or barren wasteland. Most of it is blanketed with snow for many months of the year. So learning the terrain, the layout of the land he defends, is another tremendous challenge for the aspiring fighter pilot in his Hawk.

Finland is a major overseas customer for the British

Basic flying training is completed on the L-70 Vinka (foreground) followed by the Hawk (centre), before the student pilot progresses to the Saab Draken (background) or MiG-21. PETER HOLMAN

Aerospace Hawk. BAe and Rolls-Royce marketing teams were rewarded, for their considerable efforts, in the late 1970s with a 1980 procurement of 50 Hawks followed by seven in 1993, each powered by a Rolls-Royce Turboméca Adour Mk 851 turbofan. Most of the airframes and engines were assembled in Finland by Valmet, the major aerospace/engineering/industrial group. Acquisition of the Hawk has enabled the Finnish Air Force to revise, simplify and modernise its pilot training schemes and, at the same time, its air defence tactics and strategy.

A considerable number of Hawks are based at the Air Force Academy at Kauhava in central Finland, which also handles the larger part of the Hawks' routine 300- and 600-hour airframe maintenance checks. The Hawks' introduction has enabled the Air Force to cut one level of fighter training completely with consequent savings in manpower and money, with improvements in pilots' efficiency.

"This is why the Hawk is so valuable to us", stresses the deputy commanding officer of Satakunta Wing, Lieutenant-Colonel Aarno Liusvaara. "It gives us flexibility and reliability. Our pilots need to rely heavily on instrument flying and the Hawk provides a good vehicle for this. Also the Adour's fuel consumption is low and the Hawk carries plenty of internal fuel, giving us good range without the use of wing tanks. The aircraft is extremely manoeuvrable, which is essential in the air-defence business".

At the Pirkkala base, Fighter Squadron No 21 has a total strength of just 170 personnel who between them operate and maintain four flights: operational single-seat Drakens, two-seat Drakens for supersonic interceptor training, Hawks and liaison duties.

Although small in terms of personnel the Wing is responsible for the defence of a large slice of Finland's total land area of 165,000 square miles, with seas to the west and south and Russia to the east. To the north there is little but ice and darkness to test the pilots' professionalism.

"We pride ourselves on our safety record", emphasises Major Sovelius. "Given the arduous nature of our area of operation our aircraft losses, regrettable though they are, have been kept to low numbers by a rigorous approach to safety". An exchange of information with another major operator of the Hawk, the RAF, on Hawk-related topics is cited as a contributor to this safety record. Pilots also praise the Adour turbofan for its responsiveness and robustness, while the ground technicians are pleased with its relatively simple maintenance demands. For many years to come the combination of Hawk aircraft and Adour engine will be at the heart of Finland's airborne defences, whatever the weather and whenever the season.

John Hutchinson

Ground technicians find the maintenance of the Hawk's airframe and engine relatively straightforward. PETER HOLMAN

Zimbabwe Hawk 60As of No 2 Squadron above the Victoria Falls. PETER HOLMAN

ZIMBABWE

Even at 2,000ft above Victoria Falls, turbulence generated by the thousands of tonnes of cascading water make it no easy task to keep the two Hawk aircraft straight and steady. The fact that the aircraft must drop their speed to 150kt and sit in tight behind a slow-moving CASA transport plane for a photographic shoot, only increases the buffeting and ensures that the pilots have little time to enjoy the spectacular view.

Down on the ground, visitors to one of the seven natural wonders of the world look up to watch the unexpected, free airshow as the brace of Hawks formate directly over the Falls that mark the border between Zimbabwe and Zambia. To the onlookers, the noise of the aircraft overhead is easily drowned by Mosi-oa-tunya (the smoke that thunders) – the Shona name given to the point where the mighty Zambezi River drops more than 100m into a series of narrow gorges at the rate of 12 million gal/min.

From the air, the lush, dense undergrowth that surrounds the Falls contrasts sharply with the sparser, more open plateaux that make up much of Zimbabwe. But even this vast backdrop has a welcome green tinge again, thanks to a plentiful rainy season after several years of heavy drought. A 40-minute flight over this terrain takes the two Air Force of Zimbabwe (AFZ) Hawks back to their base.

The entire Hawk fleet is assigned to No 2 Squadron, where they fulfil a multi-role requirement in ensuring the AFZ maintains its status as one of the most modern air forces in Africa. The aircraft, the first of which was delivered in 1982, are used for training, but also have an important operational capability, according to Flight Lieutenant Naison Magwa, the officer commanding 2 Squadron. "The training is in several sections. There is the fast-jet conversion, which is the students' introduction to jet aircraft. Those that are selected to stay on the Hawks go on to the squadron and join the operational conversion unit, which trains them in the operational side".

"The Hawks are also used for training the flying instructors and QWIs (Qualified Weapons Instructors)", says Flt Lt Magwa, himself a qualified instructor and

Zimbabwe's first Hawk 60 (No 600) here carrying eight 500lb BR250 bombs. BAe

operational Hawk pilot. His own basic jet training did not take place on the aircraft, however. He joined the AFZ in 1983 – the same year as the first two pilots completed their Hawk training on the squadron – but underwent his training in China and went on to fly the Chengdu F-7 for several years before transferring to the flying instructors' school.

Flt Lt Magwa joined 2 Squadron in 1992 and took over as officer commanding a year later. Since transferring to the Hawk, he has clocked up almost 600 flying hours and has

The Hawks are used to train flying and weapons instructors. BAe

been impressed by the ease with which pilots adapt to it. "I really enjoy flying it – as does everyone I know who has flown it. It is more advanced that anything else we have in the AFZ and, although there is still great affection for the other types of jet aircraft in the AFZ inventory, the Hawk is the aircraft every pilot wants to fly", he enthuses.

But while Flt Lt Magwa commands the Hawk squadron, responsibility for training lies with Squadron Leader Shebba Shumbayaonda, one of the few current members of the AFZ to have clocked up 1,000 hours on the aircraft.

Since 1988, all AFZ pilots have undergone training in Zimbabwe. This begins with six weeks in a classroom environment before going on to 130 hours of basic flying training in turboprop Gennets. The cream of the students – six at a time – are then selected for the jet flying training school, which involves 80 hours of flying spread over about four months.

"It covers a number of exercises such as general handling, navigation, night flying and instrument flying", said Sqn Ldr Shumbayaonda. "Typically, students are flying for two hours each day. After each exercise, we go into circuit flying to keep building up their confidence with the aircraft". After 16 of those 80 hours, the student experiences his first solo sortie – an accomplishment marked afterwards by the hapless individual being ceremonially doused in engine oil by his fellow trainees.

Completion of the JFTS course means students are allocated to one of the three front-line aircraft types. Those selected for the Hawk begin another 80 hours of flying in the OCU, now learning about the operational aspects of the aircraft. With the student pilot now familiar with the

Student pilots of the Air Force of Zimbabwe fly solo in the Hawk 60 after just 16 hours' instruction in the aircraft. PETER HOLMAN

No 612, one of five Mk 60As delivered in 1992, has the more powerful Adour 861A. PETER HOLMAN

aircraft, this second 80 hour section takes an average of three months. Flt Lt Magwa explains: "The Hawks have a varied role operationally, covering interdiction, air-to-air, ground support and more specialised duties such as escorts and ceremonial flypasts and displays".

Completion of the OCU section is normally required before a pilot can be considered for instructing duties. As Sqn Ldr Shumbayaonda explains: "We would want to see instructors who are also operationally capable".

In the early days of the AFZ's Hawk training operations, student throughput was limited to four at a time. This increased to the current six with the arrival of a second batch of aircraft in 1992. The five new aircraft are designated Mk 60As – slightly uprated versions of the original Mk 60s, for which the AFZ was the an early customer. The new aircraft are powered by the Adour 861A.

This version of the Hawk has an enhanced operational capability and allows it to play a fuller role in the air defence of the country, a role which Air Commodore Ian Harvey, Director General of Operations, based at the AFZ headquarters in the capital, Harare, explains: "The primary role of the AFZ is to defend Zimbabwe's airspace. The Hunter has given us sterling service since 1962 and the Hawk has come in and carried on in that tradition. It has very much come in as 'Son of Hunter'. "The big advantage is that it is independent of ground equipment for starting, so it can operate from all the private runways in the country. That means it can be quickly deployed to other bases we keep the mothballed for military use and pressed into service if needed".

As a land-locked country with four borders – Zambia, Mozambique, South Africa and Botswana – Zimbabwe's ability to defend its airspace is paramount. With the Hawk 60s' combat range of 620 miles, fully armed and a four-hour airborne endurance up to 115 miles from base, these mothballed airfields ensure the AFZ can quickly intercept any threat along its borders, stresses Air Commodore

Harvey, adding: "Zimbabwe is hot and high but it does not affect the Hawk, that is remarkably at home at our altitudes and temperatures". The aircraft operates from airfields at altitudes up to 5,000ft and in temperatures up to 35°C.

Responsibility for ensuring that the Hawks and their Adour powerplants cope with Zimbabwe's climate is Sqn Ldr Charles Maradzike, OC Technical Wing. His job is to provide sufficient aircraft to allow 2 Squadron and the instructors to carry out their flying requirements. On the squadron itself, a 30-strong ground crew is responsible for the day-to-day preparation of the Hawks and for their pre-flight checks, inspection and first-line maintenance. In charge of this ground crew is Warrant Officer Mike Raphael, who has six members of his team looking after the Adour engines, which he describes as "Very reliable. We have very few problems with them".

Entrance qualifications for prospective engineers to today's AFZ are very stringent, just as they are for potential pilots. The minimum standard is two science A levels, but in a country that sets great store by education, higher qualifications are more usual. New maintenance recruits spend the first months of their training at the Technical School in Harare, explained WO Raphael, before they are assigned to a squadron where the training continues on the job, working with qualified personnel.

Because of the hot Zimbabwe climate – although there can be early morning frosts in the winter months and there is a rainy season around February time – the day at the base starts early. As the sun rises, the 2 Squadron ground crew is pushing back the hangar doors and preparing the Hawks for another day's flying. Meanwhile the pilots and students go through pre-flight briefing in readiness for the day's sorties.

A similar pattern of working hours is to be found at the AFZ's Manyame base, alongside Harare International Airport. It is at Manyame that the second-line-maintenance of the Adours is carried out and where an engine test-bed is

A Hawk 60 being prepared for a day's flying in the 'hot and high' conditions for much of the year in Zimbabwe. PETER HOLMAN

nearing completion.

Wing Commander Elijah Chingosho is the officer commanding the base technical wing, responsible for maintenance on the Hawks and Adours as well as the CASA, Islander and Dakota fixed-wing aircraft stationed at Manyame, together with the fleets of Bell and Alouette helicopters. "With the parts to hand, we can maintain or overhaul an Adour very quickly because of its modular design. We have developed a corps of experienced technicians on the engine and the documentation for it is very clear. We follow that very closely and never make any modifications".

It is that attention to the technical details which is one of the things that has impressed Geoff Marshall, Rolls-Royce's service representative based in Harare. He says: "The AFZ has a very high level of quality control in its maintenance. If the engineers are not happy or sure about the work they have done, they do not let the engine go back on the flight line – and that attitude is to be applauded".

One of the projects Geoff has been following closely, since arriving in Zimbabwe, is the building of a fully calibrated engine test-bed at Manyame. Once operational, it will not only cater for the domestic Adour fleet but will also

be capable of providing a service for other operators in the region – including Kenya, which has 12 Hawk Mk 53s powered by the Adour 851 – thereby enhancing still further the AFZ's reputation as a leading Hawk operator.

John Oliver

The maintenance of the Hawks and their Adour powerplants is carried out by the AFZ at Manyame. PETER HOLMAN

SWITZERLAND

The first Swiss Air Force Hawk T66 flying with a Vampire Trainer, that it was to replace. BAe

The elegant swept-wing shape of the British Aerospace Hawk is an increasingly familiar sight in the skies above pilot training bases of air forces around the world. One of the nations to complete delivery of its Hawks and to put them into service is Switzerland, where the type has replaced a British designed jet trainer of an earlier era, the de Havilland Vampire.

The Vampire, and the de Havilland Venom, which was also operated by the Swiss Air Force, had another aspect in common with the Hawk: like the new trainer they were acquired in considerable numbers for miliary pilot training around the world. The Vampire and the Hawk were also ordered 'off the drawing board' by the British Ministry of Defence – a signal of confidence in the designers that was to prove well founded.

Switzerland made the decision in 1987 to take this latest generation of British trainer aircraft after intensive evaluation of competing types. A vital part of the procurement package was the requirement that Swiss industry must be involved directly. As a result, work worth some 60 million francs has been undertaken in the country.

Deliveries of 20 aircraft began in January 1990, when the first Mk 66 Hawk landed at the Swiss Air Force training academy at Sion, in the south-west of Switzerland. This aircraft was to be the sole British-built Hawk in the Swiss fleet, having been assembled at BAe's Kingston and Dunsfold facilities and equipped in the UK with the export version of the Adour, the Mk 861A of 5,700lb take-off thrust.

All but the first of the Swiss Air Force Hawks were assembled and test flown in Switzerland. PETER HOLMAN

Delivery of this, the last of the 20 Swiss Hawk T66s (U-1270), was completed on time in October 1991. PETER HOLMAN

The following 19 Hawks were manufactured jointly by BAe and Swiss industry, with assembly and test flying undertaken at the Federal Aircraft Factory in Emmen. The Adour Mk 861A-03 engines were assembled by Sulzer Brothers in Switzerland. Seven major Swiss sub-contractors and several other local companies were also involved in the programme. The Mk A-03 has the same performance as the Mk A, but incorporates detail changes to meet Swiss Air Force requirements.

Delivery of these aircraft was completed on schedule in October 1991, when General Werner Jung, commander-in-chief of the Swiss Air Force, accepted the documentation of the final Hawk in a ceremony at Sion. General Jung and other senior Swiss personnel praised the long experience of Rolls-Royce and British Aerospace and the strong support which they gave in the selection and procurement phases of the Hawk.

The decision to replace the Vampires – many of which dated from the late 1940s – was taken in 1984 and the four types of jet trainer that were then deemed the best available were subsequently evaluated. "Our special military requirements had to be taken into account in the evaluation of each aircraft type", says Alfred Lauder, chief of section in the GRD. "By 1987 the Swiss Defence Ministry was able to present to our Parliament a request for 20 Hawks and a flight simulator".

Compared with the Vampire, the first jet for the student pilots is an advanced and modern aircraft. It has also proved a highly reliable machine. The Hawk force in its entirety has been operating for five years and, in the words of Colonel J Peyer, the Swiss Air Force officer at Emmen in charge of the introduction of the aircraft: "It has already distinguished itself in our training operations by its good reliability. Our training schedule has been influenced very positively by the Hawk's high level of availability and by the small amount of time needed to prepare the aircraft for

Compared to the Vampire, the Hawk has proved to be highly reliable and adaptable in service with the Swiss Air Force.
PETER GUNTI

The Hawk's performance and good handling characteristics are well-liked by the Swiss Air Force. F&W FOTO

New hangars and servicing bays were constructed for the Hawk. R-R/PETER HOLMAN

flight readiness".

Colonel Peyer cites many improvements in Hawk-based training compared with the previous system. These include higher performance, greater efficiency, modern aerodynamics aimed at maximum safety and good characteristics for instrument-flying training. "The Hawk has an extended training spectrum that results in savings on more expensive, more noisy and more maintenance-intensive flying hours in combat aircraft", he says.

Colonel Peyer emphasises the 'teacher-friendliness' of the Hawk from the instructor's position, singling out the extremely good visibility from both seats as being particularly valuable for pilot training. "With the Hawk, the overall efficiency and safety of our pilot training has improved considerably, helped also by the excellent Hawk simulator. All staff responsible for training are enthusiastic about the Hawk's flying characteristics".

The course for student pilots encompasses 30 weeks' work at Sion and at Emmen, where the Rediffusion-supplied Hawk simulator is based. The students enter the Hawk course with basic flying skills developed on the turboprop-powered Pilatus PC-7 Turbo-Trainer. By their sixth week, after a transition spell on the Hawk with an instructor in the rear seat, they are ready to go solo.

Students progress quickly through formation flying exercises, air-to-ground combat practice, navigation training, one-against-one air combat and finally one-against-two fighting. To ensure that they maintain the widest possible range of flying skills they carry out regular continuity training, throughout the course, on the PC-7, which has many characteristics in common with the Hawk.

The instructors at Sion are unanimous in their praise for the Hawk. "Using the old Vampire for jet flying training meant a step back for the students", says flying instructor Captain Felix Stoffel. "But now, with the Hawk, we have the most competent and effective training aircraft available". The reliability, quick throttle response and overall ease of handling of the Adour is appreciated by students and instructors alike. The turbofan's low fuel consumption

provides the Hawk with much greater range and endurance than was available from the Vampire. High on the list of aircraft plus-points are good visibility, responsive handling, a well designed cockpit and reliable systems. Sion personnel are delighted with the new aircraft also for its ease of maintenance, sensible design features and quick turnaround capability.

On the Sion flight line a row of new aircraft servicing bays, each roofed and with automatic up-and-over doors at front and rear, enables technicians to service the Hawks and make pre- and post-flight checks with impressive ease, speed and safety. Each aircraft is checked, replenished with fuel and oxygen, restarted and despatched on another training sortie within minutes.

At Sion the Air Force has at its command not only a highly efficient vehicle in which to train pilots for front-line operations in F-5 and Mirage III jets, but also a multi-role trainer that enables the Swiss to strengthen national defence capabilities with a modern two-seater.

Pilots are trained in what the Swiss refer to as 'aggressive defence' – a use of arms that has deterred invaders of this neutral country since 1815. In a rapidly changing European defence climate, Switzerland's Hawk force is set to play an important and doubtless long-term role in maintaining an efficient support to its army.

John Hutchinson

The Sion based Hawks are providing the Swiss Air Force with a cost-effective trainer for the country's air defence pilots. R-R/PETER HOLMAN

UNITED STATES

Goshawk country – *NAS Kingsville is home to the US Navy's fleet of T-45As of Training Wing 2.* R-R/ANDREW SIDDONS

The mid-afternoon temperature has long since passed 100°F, while the almost-total humidity seems to suck all the oxygen straight from your lungs. The sun beats mercilessly on the concrete apron and surrounding hangars; the oppressive heat is only reinforced by the Force 7 wind that blows straight off the sun-baked Texas prairie many miles inland. This is Goshawk Country.

All around, jets in the distinctive markings of US Navy trainer aircraft jockey for position between apron and runway. The steady flow of take-offs is interspersed with jets already airborne on circuit-and-bump training: approaching the runway, touching down briefly before soaring again into the painfully bright sky. This typical level of daily activity begins at first light and continues through to well after sundown at Naval Air Station Kingsville. Situated just along the Gulf of Mexico coast from the elegant Texan city of Corpus Christi, Kingsville is home not only to the first two Goshawk trainer squadrons, but also to a whole new training system – the T45TS.

Late in 1994, the first ten US Navy and Marine Corps students to earn their wings on the T-45A Goshawk passed

Student pilot climbing into a T-45A on the busy apron, prior to a solo training sortie, at Kingsville. R-R/ANDREW SIDDONS

out from the base after a nine-month training attachment to VT-21 Squadron. In that time, they clocked up around 175 flying hours during 120 sorties, culminating with the ultimate test for any would-be naval aviator – putting the aircraft down on the thin strip of deck of a US Navy carrier.

While the McDonnell Douglas/British Aerospace Goshawk is significantly different from the BAe Hawk, from which it is derived, the truly revolutionary aspect of Kingsville's T45TS programme is to be found on the ground. The aircraft is just one part of an integrated training system that also includes advanced flight simulators, instructional programmes using computer-assisted techniques, a computerised training integration system and a logistics support package operated by the prime contractor, McDonnell Douglas Aerospace. Never before have future pilots learned their craft through a totally-integrated package. The TS in T45TS stands for Training System and from the earliest days of the first student intake in January 1994, the system has won nothing but praise from instructors and students alike.

Captain Steven Counts is the commander of Training Wing 2 at Kingsville, putting him in charge of aircraft in the base's two flying squadrons as well as the Strike Instructor Training School. A qualified navy pilot for almost 25 years, Captain Counts is impressed by the results that were being achieved as soon as the first T45TS students arrived towards the end of 1993. "I had never seen an integrated system before, and boy this is the way to go. The benefits seem almost endless – almost every day we are seeing new ones. We can do so much more with this system; it just expands the window of opportunity".

Captain Counts' enthusiasm is matched by that of the chief flying instructor, Commander Bill 'Montana' Dubois, a veteran navy flier with almost 9,000 flying hours – over 5,000 of them as an instructor – in a career spanning more than 30 years. He joined NAS Kingsville in 1980 and first flew the Goshawk in January 1992. Since then, Commander Dubois has needed little convincing that the programme is an improvement on previous training systems, despite its long and occasionally painful gestation. "I'm very happy with the whole system, even though we are still learning. It gives us a new way to train students through the electronic classroom and computer-aided instruction – and it appears we are getting a better product faster", he enthuses. "In the Goshawk, the Navy has, for the first time, a pure trainer".

The aircraft has been extensively developed from the Hawk 60, to allow it to operate from aircraft carriers. Modifications included strengthened fuselage and landing gear and the addition of a nose tow launching bar and an arrester hook. These changes, along with additional navigation and communication equipment, increased the aircraft's all-up weight, leading to the need for a more powerful version of the Rolls-Royce Turboméca Adour engine, designated the F405-RR-401, that delivers 5,845lb of thrust.

The real culture change provided by the T45TS is on the ground, where the latest in computer-generated technology provides a level and depth of pre-flight instruction, explanation and experience never before seen in a training syllabus. The 175 flying hours that each student undertakes are preceded by 81 hours in a classroom environment and 98 hours in the flight simulators. There is also a further 155 hours of specific flight briefings, the only time, apart from actual flying, where students and instructors are one-to-one.

The typical student/instructor ratio on the ground is three-to-one for each of the 12 modules that make up the programme, each module tackling a specific aspect of training. Much of the early classroom work is given over to instilling a comprehensive knowledge of the aircraft cockpit and systems. Such familiarisation is considerably aided by the giant projection screens behind the instructor, which can show a 3-D view from the cockpit for every conceivable flight situation.

The value of these screens is augmented by the students' access to individual terminals that are also 3-D, allowing trainees to go through each flying mission in minute detail to ensure they fully understand what is expected of them. Where this approach has paid off most spectacularly is in the more advanced stages of the programme, covering weapons training and air-manoeuvrability.

"I can't even begin to describe the difference", says Commander Dubois giving his first reaction on the difference the T45TS approach has made to the initial ground weapon delivery aspect of the course. "Previously, the instructor in the classroom would try to describe manoeuvres using models in each hand. The first flying sortie was invariably hopeless as no one knew what to do. Now, they have interactive videos that give a 3-D picture of

Student pilot and instructor in T-45A Goshawk 163612 lifting off from the runway on a dual training flight. R-R/ANDREW SIDDONS

At Kingsville, student pilots become familiar with the handling characteristics of the T-45A Goshawk, before embarking on the demanding phases of flight training aboard carriers at sea. R-R/ANDREW SIDDONS

every manoeuvre and students tend to go straight out and fly and hit the target". A further advantage of a classroom-based facility, allied to a comprehensive simulator set-up, is when a student is having difficulty mastering any particular aspect of the training, it provides a safe and cost-effective method of learning. This approach, allied to a very careful initial selection procedure, means the drop-out rate for US Navy jet pilots is very low.

"Previously, an awful lot of people fell out along the way. Those that survived did pretty well", remarks Commander Dubois. "Today, when we recruit, we take those we think have the desire, motivation and ability to succeed and we make every effort to allow them to excel". This view is endorsed by Lieutenant Tana Jay Tacoosin, one of Kingsville's 17 instructor pilots on the T-45A. She says: "One of the toughest things facing the students is the decision-making process. For instance, from very early on in the course, they choose how they are going to manage their fuel on each sortie. "The syllabus is designed always to be hard. Every time they start to feel comfortable, we throw

something else at them". Each flight, whether solo or accompanied, is preceded by a thorough briefing, typically two hours for a one to one-and-a-half-hour sortie, and concludes with a debrief lasting up to an hour.

For instructors and students alike, flying is still an exhilarating experience, thanks to the fast, light and easily-manoeuvrable jet. Those characteristics, allied to its forgiving nature and low stalling speed, mean the Goshawk has replaced both the Navy's T-2C Buckeye basic jet trainer and the TA-4J Skyhawk advanced jet trainer. Students now come to the T45TS programme straight from 60 hours on the T-34C Mentor turboprop, which is due to be replaced by the Joint Primary Aircraft Training System (JPATS) by the end of the decade.

Compared to the A-4 the T-45 can be turned round in just 30 minutes (half the time of the A-4). This fast turnround time is the responsibility of programme prime contractor McDonnell Douglas, which has a sizeable team at Kingsville maintaining the Goshawks and the ground-based training equipment. Such an arrangement is another

Above and below: *Goshawks with solo pilots being prepared for catapult launches from the USS* Carl Vinson. MDC

this a sensible use of American taxpayers' money, it also allows the Navy to get on with its primary role on the base – teaching pilots to fly fast jets.

In these days of defence budgets permanently under political scrutiny, the T45TS is allowing the Navy to maintain its required high standards while delivering measurable operational savings, such as in the use of simulators. Far more than just a glorified arcade game, the Hughes Simulation System provides pilots with a thorough feel of what they will experience in the air, without the inevitable expense of actually flying. "You want to be able to make mistakes without danger. The simulator takes some of the tension off and gives students some mental pictures of what things look like. It does nothing but enhance the learning curve, and the steeper you can get that, the cheaper the training is. That's the reality of things today", comments Commander Dubois.

As more aircraft have been delivered to the base, the flying hours have risen dramatically. For the 1995 financial year (October 1994-September 1995), they were over 33,000 – 61 hours for each aircraft a month. Among the first ten students, who are now 'winged' and have moved on to

example of the path T45TS is pioneering. Almost the only contact the instructors and trainees have with the aircraft is when they go on to the apron prior to take-off. Not only is

Going for the third wire, the T-45A Goshawk in its demanding environment operating from a US Navy training carrier at sea.

The US Navy is building up to train 165 student pilots a year at Kingsville on the T-45A. R-R/ANDREW SIDDONS

operational squadrons, was student naval aviator Dan Bare. He was also one of the transitional students who went through the T-2 training prior to the T45TS. Speaking two-thirds of the way through the nine month course, his views bore out Commander Dubois' assessment: "The programme is the most challenging thing I've ever done, but it's the most rewarding as well. "By this stage, I'm trying not to be a student but a pilot. Every time I walk into a briefing room, I know what is expected of me".

That self-confidence, which must never spill over into arrogance, had obviously grown during the course as Dan Bare recalled his first carrier landing in the T-2 on the USS *Eisenhower* in the Gulf of Mexico. "It was awesome. When you first approach the ship, you think you'll never be able to land on it. But afterwards, there's just this incredible sense of achievement". A fellow student on that first course was US Marine Corps First Lieutenant Chris Ghee, who could recall his feelings the first time he flew the T-45A: "It's pretty intimidating at first as it was so much faster that anything I had experienced before. You have to think so much quicker".

VT-21 Squadron, that took the first T45TS students, received its full complement of Goshawks during that first course and has now been joined in the programme by its immediate neighbour at Kingsville, VT-22, whose A-4s have transferred to Meridian Naval Air Station in Mississippi. Once all 72 aircraft due at Kingsville have arrived from McDonnell Douglas' facility at St Louis in Missouri, Meridian itself is scheduled to start up an identical T45TS programme. That is set for 1996, but the Meridian aircraft will feature the digital Cockpit 21, an almost identical layout to the Navy's main front-line fighter, the F/A-18 Hornet. Retrofitting of that advanced cockpit in

Kingsville's aircraft will commence once Meridian's T45TS programme is fully operational.

At the Texas base, the Navy is planning to train 165 students a year in seven or eight courses. Most would-be jet pilots – an increasing number of whom are female – join the service straight from college. The upper age limit is 27. Only when a significant database of flying has been built up and studied will the instructors, and the Navy as a whole, be able to finally gauge all the benefits the T45TS programme is delivering.

In the meantime, Commander Dubois is willing to offer a glowing personal assessment based on his experience to date: "I like the plane and I like the system; it's a quantum leap over what we have had in the past and we haven't even begun to see the capabilities. I think the T-45A will become legendary in naval aviation".

John Oliver

The end of another busy day at Kingsville. MDC

NEW GENERATION

Production Hawk 103 for the Royal Air Force of Oman, accompanied by the Hawk 200 RDA (Radar Development Aircraft).
BAe/CHRIS RYDING

The latest additions to the Hawk family of military aircraft are the Hawk 100 two-seat fighter and advanced weapons systems training aircraft and, the single-seat, radar-equipped, Hawk 200. Both aircraft were developed as private ventures by British Aerospace and both have achieved significant export success around the world.

HAWK 100

If the Hawks of the *Red Arrows* aerobatic team, are the most visible element of the United Kingdom Hawk fleet, then the Hawk 100 is surely the most visible of all export variants of Hawk. Two world tours and a host of air show appearances have convincingly demonstrated the outstanding reliability and operational flexibility of this latest variant.

The Hawk 100 is a development of the earlier Hawk 60 Series aircraft, and began life in the early 1980s as the Hawk EGA (Enhanced Ground Attack), with Venezuela seen as a potential launch customer for the type. Sadly, this deal fell through, but work on the project was allowed to continue and the Hawk 100 subsequently emerged. As with the Hawk 200, design staff at Kingston-upon-Thames had realised that the future export potential of Hawk could be realised

by providing the aircraft with more power, an enhanced weapons capability and a realistic night/adverse weather capability, through the use of advanced sensor systems such as forward looking infra-red (FLIR) and laser ranging.

British Aerospace's Hawk demonstrator aircraft (ZA101) was modified to serve as the Hawk 100 prototype. It is shown here on its maiden flight from Dunsfold on 1 October 1987. BAe

Hawk 100 ZA101 during an early test flight, fitted with two 190gal (860lit) tanks on the inboard pylons, two 100lb (50kg) bombs on the outboard pylons and a centreline Aden gun pod. BAe/GEOFF LEE

Hawk 100 ZA101 in dedicated air defence role, with four AIM-9 Sidewinder missiles and a 30mm Aden gun pod. BAe/GEOFF LEE

To accommodate these sensors, minor modification to the standard Hawk nose profile would be necessary and, in late-1986, British Aerospace's Hawk demonstrator aircraft, ZA101, was suitably modified to serve as the Hawk 100 prototype. Equipped with a lengthened nose profile for aerodynamic assessment and eventual provision for FLIR and laser sensors, this new Hawk variant took to the air for the first time on 1 October 1987, from Dunsfold airfield.

From then on, until November 1988, when the aircraft transferred to the Flight Test and Development Centre at Warton, ZA101 undertook a series of weapons carriage trials and customer demonstration flights, aimed at proving the operational flexibility of this new variant. To underline the reliability and integrity of the new Hawk 100, in late-September 1988, British Aerospace despatched ZA101, in company with the Hawk 200 demonstrator ZH200, to Australia, to participate in the Bi-Centennial Air Show at RAAF Richmond. ZA101 and ZH200 flew unescorted, in eleven stages, to Australia, with all en route support provided by the pilots themselves. With their Australian commitments fulfilled, the two aircraft then undertook a tour of the Far East, finally arriving back at Warton on 14

November 1988. At the conclusion of the tour, ZA101 had accumulated 104 flight hours, in 69 sorties, and had flown over 23,000 miles with absolute reliability throughout.

In 1989 ZA101 went into the hangars at Warton, for the installation of the newly-developed, seven-station combat wing and an uprated Adour Mk 871 turbofan engine developing 5,845lb st. The analogue instrumentation of earlier Hawk variants was retained on ZA101, and it was not until 29 February 1992, that the first definitive 100 Series aircraft (ZJ100) was flown.

ZA101 emerged from the flight development hangars at Warton, in early 1990 and resumed flight testing on 27 April, albeit in a dreadful mixture of original weathered white paint and yellow primer. Later in the year ZA101 entered the spray shops at Warton and re-emerged in a Middle Eastern style camouflage scheme, in readiness for further weapons carriage trials and an appearance at the Farnborough Air Show. ZA101 continued to provide valuable service to the Hawk 100 Series development programme until February 1995, when it was withdrawn from flight status. In the interim, however, the aircraft had been used for flight envelope expansion, CRV-7 rocket

Hawk 100 and 200 flying over the Sydney Opera House whilst attending the Bi-centennial Air Show at RAAF Richmond in September 1988. BAe

Fitted with the new seven-station combat wing and more powerful Adour 871, Hawk 100 ZA101 was airborne again on 27 April 1990. BAe

ZA101 was re-painted in desert camouflage for its appearance at Farnborough in September 1990. BAe/GEOFF LEE

ZA101 undertook weapons trials with CRV-7 rocket pods before being withdrawn from operational service in February 1995.
BAe/CHRIS RYDING

Hawk 100/102D ZJ100 was first flown from Warton on 29 February 1992. It had the full avionic, flight control and structural modifications. BAe

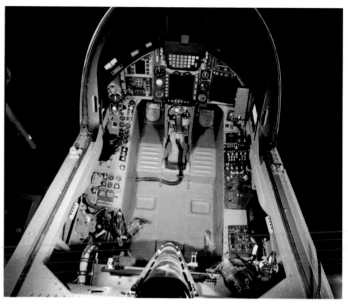

Photograph showing the spacious and well laid out digital front cockpit of a Hawk 100 series aircraft. BAe

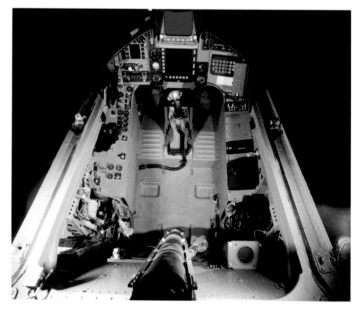

The rear cockpit of a Hawk 100 showing the repeater display of the FLIR/HUD. Its associated data entry panel is on the right of the main instrument panel and below the FLIR/HUD is the multi-purpose display (MPD). BAe

firing trials and even for staff pilot continuation training. In 1992 it had embarked on a further round of globe trotting, this time appearing at the Singapore Air Show and making customer demonstration flights in the Far East, India and the Middle East.

Today, much of the development work on the Hawk 100 programme is undertaken by ZJ100, better known to British Aerospace staff as the Hawk 102D. ZJ100 was the first 100 Series aircraft to fly with the full range of avionic and structural modifications and has yielded valuable data for the Hawk development team.

The Hawk 100 is a two-seat fighter and advanced weapons systems training aircraft, with secondary ground attack capability. Principal features of the aircraft are:- the lengthened nose profile with provision for FLIR and laser sensors, advanced cockpit layouts with multi-function displays (MFDs) and hands-on-throttle-and-stick (HOTAS) controls; an advanced avionics system with principal elements linked through a MIL-STD-1553B databus; a seven-station combat wing with combat manoeuvre flaps, and an uprated Adour Mk 871 turbofan engine. For self-protection, the aircraft is equipped to carry wingtip-mounted air-to-air missiles, a fin-mounted radar warning receiver (RWR) and chaff/flare dispensers located on the rear fuselages above the jet pipe. Data from the RWR is projected on to the pilot's HUD.

Principal elements of the Hawk 100 avionic system are:- the LINS 300 laser inertial navigation system; new generation Smiths Industries HUD/weapon aiming computer (WAC) and, a new, highly-accurate air data sensor (ADS). Operational data is presented to the crew on full-colour, head-down MFDs and, for improved capability at night and in adverse weather, each cockpit is equipped with a FLIR display. In the front cockpit this is situated at the right side of the main instrument console, whilst in the

rear cockpit, the unit is located centrally, above the MFD. For reduced aircrew workload in a combat environment, both cockpits are equipped with HOTAS controls, whereby all time-critical weapon control switches are ergonomically grouped on the throttle and control stick.

As an operational aircraft, the Hawk 100 can undertake a wide variety of operational missions, including air defence, close air support, interdiction and reconnaissance, as well as advanced training missions. It can also carry an extensive range of external stores on four under-wing pylons and a single under-fuselage pylon, in addition to the air-to-air missiles that are carried on the wingtip pylons. The two inboard pylons are equipped to carry 130 Imp Gal fuel tanks, and all four wing pylons can be equipped with twin-store carriers. Weapon options include rocket pods, freefall bombs, retarded and cluster bombs, air-to-air missiles and a range of reconnaissance and ECM (electronic countermeasures) pods. A 30mm Aden gunpod can also be carried on the fuselage centreline. As with the Hawk 200, maximum stores capacity is 6,000lb and weapons are selected for releases via the weapons control panel (WCP), situated at the upper left side of the front and rear

The Hawk 102D left the UK on 30 October 1993 for a 40,000 mile demonstration tour to Australia. BAE/CHRIS RYDING

Painted in tactical brown and green camouflage, Hawk 102D ZJ100 is seen flying over Qatar in the United Arab Emirates during its 1993 World Tour. BAe/GEOFF LEE

instrument consoles. In keeping with earlier variants of Hawk, the Hawk 100 retains its carefree handling characteristics in all regimes of flight, even when heavily armed.

In late-1993, considerable export potential in the Middle East, Far East, India and Australia, prompted British Aerospace to undertake a second Hawk world tour, on this occasion utilising Hawk 102D, ZJ100, painted in a pseudo-South East Asian paint scheme, as the demonstrator aircraft. In company with a BAe146-300 support aircraft, and a small team of engineers and marketing personnel, ZJ100 left Warton on Saturday 30 October to begin a gruelling 52-day tour to Australia and back. During the 47 flying days of the tour, ZJ100 made 92 flights – made up of 42 VIP demonstration flights, 22 aerobatic displays and 28 ferry flights – and covered a staggering 40,000 miles. Yet for all this effort, aircraft maintenance was confined to just one set of main wheel brake pads, two sets of tyres and 4-litres of engine oil. Faced with facts like these, it is little wonder that Hawk 100 has, to date, outsold all of its principal competitors, and looks set to do so for many years to come.

HAWK 200
The Hawk 200 was the first of this operational pair to fly, having made its maiden flight on 19 May 1986, in the hands of test pilot, Mike Snelling. With the Hawk 200, it really was a case of third time lucky, as two previous attempts to develop the aircraft, had been thwarted by a lack of funding.

The idea of developing a single-seat variant of the Hawk

The prototype Hawk 200 was first flown on 19 May 1986. BAe

first took root in the mid-1970s at Kingston, as part of the on-going design philosophy. Pilots who had evaluated the Hawk T1, began to remark on the aircraft's excellent handling characteristics, describing them as more akin to a front line combat aircraft than an advanced trainer. The Hawk's rugged airframe, combined with its high subsonic speed, excellent manoeuvrability, long range and useful weapons carrying capability, gave it considerable operational potential and one way to exploit that potential was through a single-seat variant that would compliment the two-seat trainer.

Initial studies carried out in the mid-1970s, had the cockpit of the single-seater, situated between the two crew positions of the standard Hawk, thereby allowing additional space in the nose for avionic equipment and additional space aft of the cockpit for more fuel. The new cockpit position would be sufficiently raised to provide adequate all-round vision, and rear vision would be enhanced by the incorporation of a bubble-type canopy. A variety of equipment fits were considered, ranging from a simple Doppler-twin gyro platform navigation system and gyro gunsight, to a Doppler air intercept (AI) radar, inertial navigation system (INS), and HUD/WAC. In the end, however, no funding was available and the project was shelved.

A second attempt at developing a single seat variant was made in 1979, by which time the more powerful Adour Mk 861 (5,700lb st) had become available. On this occasion, design staff at Kingston-upon-Thames adopted a minimum change approach to the project, and proposed to leave the pilot in either the existing front or rear cockpit position of the standard Hawk. Larger drop tanks, each holding 130 Imp Gal were also now available for use with the Hawk, thus eliminating the need for costly structural changes to increase internal fuel capacity within the fuselage. The single-seater would also benefit from the aerodynamic and structural changes developed for the Hawk 60 Series. The location of the pilot in the front seat position was quickly rejected on the grounds that rearward visibility was inadequate. With the pilot located in the rear seat position, visibility was significantly improved and twin cannons could be installed in the nose. Once again, however, funding was not available for development of the aircraft, and the project was shelved for a second time.

Finally, in 1982/1983, design staff at Kingston were successful in persuading British Aerospace management that increased potential could be realised by incorporating night/adverse weather capability, a comprehensive weapons fit and a realistic self-defence capability into both the Hawk 100 and 200 variants. This time, designers located the pilot of the single-seater between the cockpit positions of the standard Hawk trainer, as this provided adequate all-round visibility, and adequate space ahead of, and beneath, the cockpit for internal guns, which were subsequently deleted

The prototype Hawk 200 ZG200 under construction at Kingston early in 1986. BAe

in favour of the ventral gun pod. The nosewheel leg was also moved slightly aft on the Hawk 200, to provide yet more space for avionic equipment. Originally, FLIR and laser sensors were considered for installation in the nose of the aircraft, but these were later abandoned in favour of an AI radar system.

With funding for the project provided in late-1983, work on the Hawk 200 proceeded rapidly and British Aerospace was able to brief potential export customers on the capabilities of the new variant. Rolled out with considerable international interest early in 1986, the prototype Hawk 200 (ZG200), made its maiden flight on 19 May 1986. But sadly during a customer demonstration flight on 2 July 1986, ZG200 was lost when BAe test pilot Jim Hawkins is believed to have fallen victim to 'g-loc', g-induced loss of consciousness. The loss of the prototype so early in its flight test programme was a bitter blow, but detailed analysis of

The first Hawk 200 was repainted in an all black scheme shortly before it was tragically destroyed on 2 July 1986. BAe

The second Hawk 200 demonstrator (ZH200) was flown on 24 April 1987. BAe/GEOFF LEE

data from the aircraft's accident data recorder showed no fault with the aircraft or its systems. On 28 August 1986, British Aerospace announced that a second Hawk 200 demonstrator was to be built and, just eight months later, on 24 April 1987, ZH200, referred to as the first pre-production Hawk 200, made its maiden flight from Dunsfold in the hands of test pilot Chris Roberts.

To date, Hawk 200 Series aircraft have entered operational service with the air forces of Oman (Mk 203) and Malaysia (Mk 208), and the type has also been ordered by the Indonesian Air Force (Mk 209). From an operational standpoint the Hawk 200 offers true multi-role capability, at a fraction of the cost of more complex front line combat aircraft. The Hawk 200's ability to carry a heavy and varied range of weapons, means that it can undertake a wide variety of missions, ranging from air defence and close air support, to interdiction and maritime support. Equipped with long-range fuel tanks, a reconnaissance pod and wingtip-mounted air-to-air missiles, the Hawk 200 can undertake long-range fighter reconnaissance missions, or can be utilised for economic exclusion zone patrol.

From a technical viewpoint, the Hawk 200 builds on the reputation of the two-seat predecessors, offering ruggedness, reliability, ease of maintenance and, most importantly, carefree handling in all regimes of flight even when heavily armed. Utilising the same Adour Mk 871 turbofan engine as its sister ship the Hawk 100, and featuring extensive structural and systems commonality with that aircraft, the Hawk 200 becomes an attractive

proposition to export customers with limited defence budgets.

Principal characteristics of the Hawk 200 are the new, single-place, forward fuselage and the new nose radome

The Hawk 200's cockpit with HUD, up-front controller, HOTAS controls, multi-purpose display, digital stores management system and radar display. BAe/CHRIS RYDING

Development of the Hawk 200 radar system was conducted in the UK using Hawk 200 ZJ201 and in the USA using a modified BAC One-Eleven airliner operated by the Westinghouse Electronic Systems Group. WESTINGHOUSE USA

which houses a Westinghouse APG-66H, multi-mode, pulse-Doppler radar. The cockpit is fully pressurised and air conditioned and the pilot is seated on a Martin Baker Mk 1OLH, rocket-assisted, zero-zero ejection seat.

The APG-66H radar is a development of the earlier APG-66 radar used in the F-16 Fighting Falcon and operates in the X-Band. The radar offers significantly improved air-to-air and air-to-surface capabilities over its predecessor. It provides ten air-to-air modes (with four additional sub-modes for air combat) and ten air-to-surface modes (with sub-modes for fixing, target detection and ranging). The radar interfaces with other elements of the Hawk 200 avionic suite, via a MIL-STD-1553B databus, and radar data is displayed to the pilot on a monochrome display

The Hawk 200 Radar Development Aircraft made its first flight on 13 February 1992. BAe

situated at the right side of the instrument console. Development of the radar was conducted, in parallel, in both the United States and the United Kingdom, using radar systems located in the modified nose of a British Aerospace One-Eleven airliner, operated by Westinghouse Electronic Systems Group. It was also fitted in the nose of Hawk 200 ZJ201, the Radar Development Aircraft (RDA), first flown on 13 February 1992 and operating from British Aerospace's Warton flight test facility. Performance of the APG-66H is described as 'impressive', against both airborne and surface targets. Typically, the radar can acquire a fighter-size target at ranges in excess of 25nm and a bomber-size target at ranges in excess of 35nm. With maritime targets, the radar can acquire a small vessel at ranges in excess of 30nm and a larger vessel at ranges in excess of 60nm – with proportional reductions depending on sea state.

The Hawk 200 cockpit has close commonality with that of the Hawk 100, making it relatively easy for a pilot to transition from one type to the other. As with the Hawk 100, principal features of the Hawk 200 cockpit are the Smiths Industries HUD, full-colour, Head-Down MFD and the WCP. The radar display is also situated at the right side of the instrument console. In order to reduce pilot workload in a combat environment, all time-critical weapon system controls are grouped on the throttle and control stick, using the HOTAS principle. The MFD is a CRT based unit, around the edge of which are 13 software-programmed push buttons, whose functions are determined by 27 individual display formats. Information displayed on the MFD includes – navigation data, systems status and attitude director indicator (ADI).

The Hawk 200 systems design is based on simplicity and reliability – and builds on experience gained with earlier variants of the aircraft. All flying controls are hydraulically powered and operated by push-pull rods. Electrical trimming is also provided in all axes and a yaw damper provides directional stability augmentation. Aircraft manoeuvrability is enhanced by the use of double-slotted flaps, which are stressed for use in air combat. Hydraulic power is provided by two independent systems, each with its own engine-driven pump and both systems power the aircraft's flying controls. In addition, the No 1 system provides power for general services such as flaps, undercarriage, airbrakes and wheelbrakes.

As an offensive aircraft, the Hawk 200 can carry an extensive array of NATO and US weapons on four underwing pylons and a single under-fuselage pylon. In addition, the aircraft carries wingtip mounted air-to-air missiles, a fin-mounted radar warning receiver (RWR) and chaff/flare dispensers in the rear fuselage above the engine jetpipe. Data from the RWR is projected on the pilot's HUD. The Hawk 200's survivability is also greatly enhanced by its small frontal area, which makes it a difficult target to

Malaysian Hawk 208s have air-to-air refuelling capability, here being tested with an RAF VC10 K3 of No 101 Sqn.

acquire and track, both visually and with radar systems. With regard to the carriage of weapons, the Hawk 200 can carry up to 11 stores at one time – utilising the wingtip stations for missiles, the under-fuselage weapons station and twin store carriers on each of the under-wing pylons. Store options include rocket pods; freefall, retarded and cluster bombs; air-to-air and air-to-surface missiles and various reconnaissance and ECM pods. The originally planned twin Aden 30mm cannon in the forward portion of the lower fuselage were deleted in 1989/90. The space created by removal of the Aden cannon and their associated feed systems allowed a redistribution of avionic boxes within the fuselage.

With a promising future, the Hawk 200 continues to be actively promoted by British Aerospace – and few would argue with the slogan 'Lightweight Fighter – Heavyweight Punch', which so aptly describes this formidable little aeroplane.

A lightweight fighter (Hawk 200) meets a heavyweight Russian (MiG-29) on friendly terms at Farnborough in 1990. BAe

ZH200 shows its extensive under-wing stores capability and at this stage additional Aden cannon in the forward fuselage. BAe

Medium-range air-to-air and short-range air-to-air missiles can be carried in the air defence role. BAe/GEOFF LEE

Hawk 200 RDA with wing-tip mounted AIM-9L Sidewinder missiles and underwing ECM pods. BAe/GEOFF LEE

THE TALONS OF HAWK

Ian Strachan, a former RAF A1 flying instructor and ETPS graduate, who was Wing Commander Flying at RAE Farnborough, and a squadron commander at A&AEE Boscombe Down during and after the Falklands war, gives his impressions of the Hawk 100.

It was ten years almost to the day since I last flew a Hawk. That was a T1A at Boscombe Down (the UK military aircraft test establishment). From my Royal Air Force experience I knew the Hawk to be a very fine advanced trainer and a pleasure to fly, so I was keen to see how it had been developed as a weapon platform.

In November 1994, I flew in the front seat of BAe's demonstrator Hawk 100, with company pilot Phil Dye in the back. Dye is experimental test pilot and project pilot for the Hawk 100 and 200 series. Compared to the T1, the cockpit differences are significant. The single-seat 200 variant has a similar cockpit layout to the front seat of the 100.

A Mil-Std 1553 databus is the heart of the system and is duplex for redundancy purposes. Feeding it are seven weapon stations, a GEC-Marconi Avionics FLIR, Smiths Industries raster HUD, two multi-function head down displays (HDDs), laser ranging, laser-gyro inertial, RWR, chaff and IR decoy dispenser. The last three may be operated together in an automatic self-protection mode, or be switched manually. The cockpit also has a small LCD digital engine display on the right front panel, and on the

left is an LCD mimic and control panel for the armament and also an LCD-based comms controller. HOTAS controls are standard, with multiple buttons and selectors on both stick and throttle.

External differences are also significant. As well as the extended nose containing the FLIR and laser (and pulse Doppler radar in the 200 variant), there are Sidewinder air-to-air missile stations on the tips (a total of four AIM-9s may be carried) and the wing is of a new design with more area, a drooped leading edge, flaps, and a 'combat flap' facility. On the sides of the rear fuselage there are two horizontal strakes below, and just ahead of, the tailplane, similar to those on the T-45A Goshawk. These assist the airflow over the tailplane and presumably add slightly to longitudinal stability. A powered rudder is installed, and the tailcone contains a brake chute, the chaff and IR decoy dispensers, and the tail warner part of the RWR (the rest of the RWR is in the fin). The Rolls-Royce Adour engine has about 20% more thrust than in the T1 and is optimised for ISA + 35ºC.

In fact, compared to the T1, the Hawk 100 and 200 are radically different aircraft, which in many ways deserve a different name. Their relationship to the T1 is that of great-grandson descended through the Hawk 50 and 60. The 100 has been in service since late 1992 (in Abu Dhabi with the UAE Air Force) and the 200 since 1994 with the Royal Air Force of Oman. Indonesia has also ordered the Hawk.

Taxiing was straightforward and directional control

The cockpit of the Hawk 100 is significantly different from the T1.
BAe

precise using differential brake; nosewheel-steering can be offered as an option in order to reduce heating of the brakes. On take-off, a couple of dabs of brake were applied to keep straight and the rudder became effective at about 40kt. Rotation at 130kt and climb using the HUD symbology was easy. Climbing between the cloud layers of an approaching warm front, some turning and rolling manoeuvres confirmed the usual good Hawk control responses, particularly the instant and rapid roll response to lateral stick. Some loops, rolls, and horizontal-eights followed, and Dye allowed me a good session of aerobatics before getting down to real work. G was presented in the form of digits on the HUD, a useful addition to the head-down presentation on a strip gauge.

The two horizontal strakes just ahead of the tailplane are similar to those on the Goshawk. BAe

In evaluating manoeuvre performance, combat flap was a Hawk feature new to me and was selected via a HOTAS throttle button. It gives 12.5º of flap for combat manoeuvring and automatically retracts at higher speeds. To test its efficiency I turned, clean, in light to moderate buffet and selected combat flap. The buffet stopped and turn rate increased, giving about a 20kt decrement at 360kt before the same level of buffet was felt again. Repeating the process the other way, turning in combat flap in light buffet, caused heavy buffet and a marked reduction of turn rate when combat flap was deselected.

Stalling and spinning were next on the agenda, and I discovered that both clean and in all-flap and gear settings the Hawk 100 was no different in its safe stalling characteristics from the T1, at least at this centre-of-gravity and with no stores. Stalls were marked by adequate buffet warning and small wing drops at a low rate of roll. Dye encouraged me to hold it in and we simply mushed down in moderate buffet without much wing drop at about 120kt (flaps and gear up). I tried a dab of rudder and this induced about a 20º wing-drop which was easily corrected with a dab the other way; and all with full back stick. Recovery from buffet on releasing the back pressure was virtually instantaneous and we then eased up to a civilised speed. Impressively safe handling at the stall.

It was difficult finding a cloud gap in which to spin, but I managed a four-turn spin and recovery, losing 9,000ft before climbing again. Recovery was very quick when opposite rudder, followed by some forward stick, was applied. BAe said later that the standard Hawk spin recovery is simply to centralise the controls. I wanted to try a 'hands-off' recovery (which the T1 will do and, according to BAe, the 100 and 200 do as well) but cloud precluded another spin. This was followed by a quick look at air-to-air missile symbology, then guns mode was selected. The 'hot line' gun sight gives a synthetic 'tracer' type display of where the rounds should be going. For pilots used to old fashioned air-to-air gunnery, this display is magic.

Then we let down for low flying, following a route planned before flight by Dye, using the flight-planning data system programmed into the aircraft system via a data cartridge. For general flying, I used the HUD with its steering bug, velocity vector, and radar altitude displays, glancing down at the route map on the HDD which gave position, track, and the preset route. As we flew over Lake Windemere in north-west England at 420kt, visibility and cloudbase were adequate, but not ideal, and we conversed about abort procedures. It became apparent that we would soon enter cloud past Ambleside, so a quick deceleration and 180° left at 360kt (a good speed for manoeuvre without too high a turn radius) took us over Grizedale Forest and back towards Morecambe Bay. Since we knew that the visibility and cloudbase were okay here, I increased speed to over 500kt to sample higher speed low-level performance.

The rear cockpit's generous dimensions and good forward view are a positive advantage. BAe

The INS was showing a wind of 32kt; turbulence was noticeable in the cockpit, but not uncomfortable. Wind velocity is continuously computed and presented in the corner of the HDD as a small vector diagram with speed digits – a useful feature.

Looking at air-to-ground weapon-aiming modes, I picked a small offshore island in Morecambe Bay as a target and set up 'bombs' on the LCD weapon panel. The bomb-fall-line on the HUD was easy to fly through the target and I 'pickled' when the release marker moved up the bomb line and overlaid the target. Guns mode was then tried, designed for the 30mm Aden cannon pod on the centreline station. Once more, it was just a question of selecting the mode, placing the aiming marker on the target, and diving down keeping it there. Fixating on the aiming marker and the target, I pressed the trigger and expended 90% of the (hypothetical) rounds in my first pass. I had missed monitoring the 'rounds remaining' box in the bottom left of the HUD. I asked Dye if there was a limited round setting – there is – and I set up bursts of 10 rounds for the next pass, which was much more under control, with three separate

bursts of 10 rounds each. What was really needed was some live bombs and rounds and a range to try them on – the strong surface wind would have been a good test for the ballistic-prediction software. Certainly the selection, aiming and firing process in the cockpit was simple and the ground stabilisation of the aiming symbols made tracking the target very straightforward, but proof of results is only from firing live weapons. The layout of the weapon-selector panel was intuitive, the LCD display giving a mimic diagram of the stores stations.

We then established communications with BAe's Warton approach controller and were vectored for a couple of ILS approaches. One was flown using the HUD and one using the glass HDD. The first was simple to fly because the dot-and-approach-bars presentation on the HUD are easy to follow, and being processed information, all you have to do is to fly the aircraft symbol to the dot and keep it there. Rolling (touch-and-go) was straightforward, and the Hawk does not drop out of the sky while feeling for the ground (I do not like 'arrivals', unless a firm landing is needed for other reasons such as short runway, night, or adverse characteristics in ground effect). The second approach was less accurate because the HDD ILS bars display raw – rather than processed – information. This took me back to my days as a Canberra Instrument Rating Examiner, and I could hear myself repeating "set the rate-of-descent and heading, don't chase the bars." If I was a Hawk customer, I would request the option of both processed and raw information on the HDD, and use the raw data only as an emergency mode.

The flight was rounded off with some visual circuits and, having satisfied Dye that I could find the end of the runway at the right speed, I essayed a full-stop landing. Dye suggested I use the brake chute, a feature not fitted to the RAF Hawks. Having put the aircraft down on the 'piano keys' at 130kt, the landing run became a non-event when I deployed the chute, stopping within about one-third of the Warton runway using hardly any brake. This is a feature from which all Hawks would benefit. Of course, to avoid cluttering a busy airfield with chutes and also having a large repacking effort, one might use it only in emergencies; but for a very small weight penalty it seems a good feature to have. On a forced landing or aborted take-off it could save an aircraft, and users of non-chute-equipped Hawks should consider a retrofit.

After the flight I sat in the rear seat and confirmed my memory of that cockpit's generous proportions and good forward view. The rear cockpit dimensions are equivalent to the 200's which is basically a 100 with only a rear seat, the longer nose providing stowage for radar as well as other avionics.

The Hawk 100 exhibits very good handling when flown clean. When the aircraft is fully armed, I cannot comment, but its roll acceleration will be less, and its speed, acceleration, and rates of climb reduced. Its potential weapons fit and avionics make it not primarily a trainer but a light combat aircraft, ideal for real attack sorties and of course for initial and continuity weapons training. With its defensive aids suite the 100/200 would be ideal in the United Nations Bosnian air-to-ground role at a fraction of the cost of some of the aircraft currently employed. With its databus and reconfigurable cockpit, the Hawk could be used to mimic more expensive aircraft for cost-effective pre-conversion training. The Hawk as a type may not be new, but the 100/200 combination is thoroughly modern and should have a good position in a more cost-conscious market-place. BAe claims operating costs as low as US$3,000 per flying hour. Whether or not this figure matches a particular customer's environment, weapons and spares policy, what is beyond dispute is that the Hawk 100/200 is cost-effective and certainly cheaper to operate than most other available attack aircraft capable of over 500kt at low level.

Ian Strachan has flown 8,500hr in over 70 types of powered aircraft and many gliders. He edits a number of sections of Jane's *Military Training and Simulation Systems.*

The Hawk 100's potential weapons fit and avionics make it an ideal multi-role light combat aircraft, as well as a full operational trainer.

BAe/RAY TROLL

LOOKING TO THE FUTURE

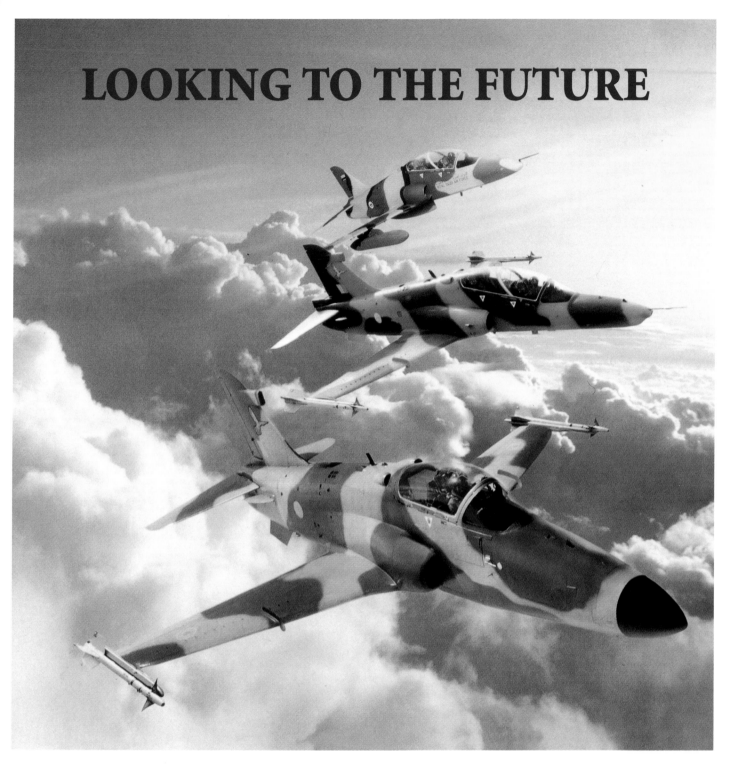

British Aerospace continues to assess customer requirements for advanced jet trainers and light combat aircraft. It remains committed to further enhancements of the Hawk family, where these are deemed to be cost-effective and exportable.

The need to integrate a wider range of advanced avionic systems and external stores is regularly reviewed, along with a range of new technologies, that might conceivably reduce still further the cost of ownership of Hawk aircraft over their extensive service lives.

Confident of a secure future for the Hawk, British Aerospace continues to market major variants of the aircraft, throughout the world, and will inevitably secure further substantial orders for the type. The Hawk World

Tour, at the end of 1993, gave a considerable boost to sales prospects in the Middle East, Far East and Australasia. One can only speculate on the volume of orders that might be generated by similar tours of Africa and Latin America, if such tours were to be organised by British Aerospace.

Nearer to home, the Royal Air Force has a pressing need for a new lead-in trainer for Eurofighter 2000 and there is a growing belief in aviation circles that Hawk 100, with its 'glass' cockpit, outstanding manoeuvrability and extensive weapons carrying capability, would be an ideal candidate for this role. Whatever the outcome, the Hawk seems set to be the world class leader in advanced trainers/light combat aircraft for many years to come.

Hawk T1 of No 100 Sqn in special display markings. BAe/GEOFF LEE

APPENDIX A
HAWK VARIANTS

Hawk T1/1A/1W

A two-seat advanced flying and weapons training aircraft. Initial production version of the Hawk. Began life as the Hawker Siddeley HS1182AJ and selected as winner of Air Staff Requirement (ASR) 397 on 1 October 1971. 176 aircraft were ordered for the Royal Air Force in March 1972. First of six pre-production aircraft (XX154) was first flown from Dunsfold airfield on 21 August 1974. It was later used for flying quality and structural load trials. The second Hawk (XX156) was the systems test aircraft and also undertook all-weather trials. The third Hawk (XX157) was used for handling, including spinning trials and the fourth (XX158) was the weapons development aircraft. Practice weapons were to be carried on the T1's two wing pylons and a 30mm gun pod could be fitted on the fuselage centreline. XX159 and XX160, the fifth and sixth Hawks, were based at A&AEE Boscombe Down for additional trials work. XX161, the first production Hawk T1 for the RAF, was used for the final Hawk engineering acceptance by the MoD(PE) and RAF prior to Service Release, before being delivered on 22 December 1976.

XX161, the first production Hawk T1. HSA

The second and third production Hawk T1s (XX162 and XX163) were the first of the type handed over to the RAF at No 4 FTS, Valley, on 4 November 1976. Hawk T1s were initially used to train flying instructors by the CFS detachment at Valley, before they replaced Gnats for student pilot advanced flying training. Eighty-eight Hawk T1s were subsequently modified by British Aerospace, between 1983 and 1986, to carry AIM-9 Sidewinder air-to-air missiles for second line defence of UK installations – they were redesignated as Hawk T1As. These aircraft were delivered to the Tactical Weapons Units at Brawdy and Chivenor where they replaced Hunters.

Between 1989 and 1993, 83 aircraft were re-winged for life extension, after the identification of fatigue cracking problems on a ground test specimen. A further 59 aircraft are due to be re-winged by mid-1995.

Sidewinder equipped Hawk T1As in 1991, operating with No 2 Tactical Weapons Unit at RAF Chivenor. BAe

Customer: Royal Air Force (T1).
Technical Data
Length overall (inc probe): 38ft 10in (11.85m);
Wing span: 30ft 10in (9.39m);
Wing area: 179.64sq ft (16.69m²)
Height overall: 13ft 2in (4.00m);
Basic mass empty: 8,000lb (3,636kg)
Take off weight (clean): 11,100lb (5,035kg)
Maximum take off weight: 12,566lb (5,700kg)
Maximum level speed (at altitude): Mach 0.9
Maximum Mach number: Mach 1.2
Maximum load factors: +8g to -4g
Ferry range: 1,500 nm
Powerplant: Rolls-Royce/Turboméca Adour Mk 151 turbofan (5,200lb st).

The Hawk 50 had additional underwing weapon pylons and revised tail cone. BAe

Hawk Mk 50 Series

Two-seat advanced flying and weapons training aircraft with ground attack capability. Initial export variant of the Hawk. Eighth production Hawk aircraft built as a company-funded demonstrator and given civil registration G-HAWK – but subsequently allocated military serial ZA101 to permit its use for weapon trials. The Hawk 50 series exploited growth potential of the Hawk design and introduced ground attack capability. First flown 17 May 1976.

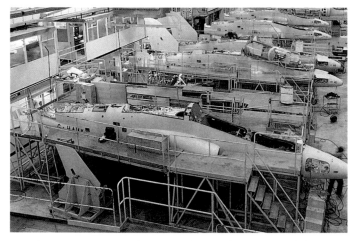

Hawk 50 G-HAWK on the T1 production line at Dunsfold. HSA

Hawk 50 en route to the Paris Air Show in 1979. BAe

Principal features of the Hawk 50 Series:-
• Uprated Rolls-Royce/Turboméca Adour Mk 851 turbofan (5,340lb st)
• Revised tailcone shape for improved directional stability
• Two additional underwing weapons pylons
• Enhanced cockpit instrumentation (including angle of attack indicator, twin gyro attitude/heading reference

The company demonstrator Hawk 50, in military markings, for weapons testing – here firing 2.57in rocket projectiles. BAe

system (AHRS) and weapons control panel for the four wing pylons and fuselage centreline station)
• Re-profiled ejection seat head boxes, for enhanced rearward visibility (now fitted to the T1/T1A).

Compared to the Hawk T1, the Hawk 50 Series has:
• Maximum operating weight increased by 30%
• Maximum disposable load increased by 70%
• Fuel load increased by 53%
• Maximum ferry range increased by 30%

Weapons carried on four underwing pylons, each of which can be configured for single or twin-store carriage. The two inboard pylons are 'wet', and can carry 100 Imp gal (455 litres) fuel tanks for additional range and endurance. The fuselage centreline pylon can be utilised for carriage of a 30mm Aden gun pod – or a range of conventional ordnance.
Customers: Finland(Mk 51/51A), Kenya (Mk 52) and Indonesia (Mk 53).

Technical data
As Hawk T1, but with a maximum take off weight of 17,085lb (7,750kg).

T-45A Goshawk
A two-seat carrier qualification and training aircraft for the United States Navy, jointly developed and produced by British Aerospace and McDonnell Douglas. McDonnell Douglas builds the forward fuselage of the aircraft and carries out final assembly at St Louis, Missouri, while British Aerospace builds all of the remaining structure, aft of the rear cockpit bulkhead. The canopy and windscreen are manufactured by Aerostructures Limited at Hamble.

On 19 November 1981, a Hawk derivative was selected

The first T-45A shows its taller fin and rudder and large ventral fin ahead of the arrester hook; two of the modifications introduced to improve handling. MDC

from five other competing designs as outright winner of the US Navy's VTXTS competition, for a new Undergraduate Pilot Training System to replace both the T-2C Buckeye and TA-4J Skyhawk. Full scale development of the aircraft began in October 1984, with work on the first two aircraft commencing in February 1986. The first T-45A (Bu No 162787) made its maiden flight on 16 April 1988 but was later lost in a landing accident at Edwards Air Force Base. The original production plan called for 54 land-based T-45B Goshawks, to be followed by 253 carrier-capable T-45As. However, in FY 1984, the T-45B was cancelled and all effort was concentrated on the T-45A. The first production T-45A was handed over to the US Navy on 23 January 1992, over two years later than scheduled, because of changes to the aircraft incorporated at the direction of the US Navy.

Initial design features of the T-45A:
• Deepened forward fuselage to accommodate the new, twin-wheel, nose oleo
• Revised cockpit layout, for greater compatibility with US Navy combat aircraft
• Strengthened fuselage and wing structure
• New undercarriage to withstand catapult-assisted take-off and high sink rate arrested carrier landings
• Arrester hook
• New side-mounted speed brakes
• Strengthened engine casing to withstand additional loads.
• Faster engine acceleration following 'wave-off' (missed approach) or 'bolter' (failure to engage the arrester wire).

Alleged performance deficiencies identified by the US Navy Operational Testing and Evaluation in 1988 became known as the 'Big Five' and led to further modifications to the aircraft. The T-45A was considered to be underpowered in high ambient temperatures, had unsatisfactory carrier approach characteristics, and had a tendency to drop a wing at the stall. In addition, the aircraft was considered to lack control harmony and exhibited unsatisfactory pitch changes when its speed brakes were deployed.

Solutions to the alleged deficiencies were as follows:
Lack of thrust was overcome by installing an uprated Adour Mk 871 engine (5,845lb st), in place of the originally specified Adour Mk 861 engine (derated from 5,700lb st). *Satisfactory 'carrier approach'* characteristics were achieved by adding six inches to the fin height; a larger ventral fin ahead of the arrester hook and fine tuning the yaw damper below 217kt. In addition the aileron gearing was changed, a rudder lock mechanism was installed and an interconnection between the aileron and rudder was introduced.
Wing stall was resolved by adding square wing tips and a full span leading edge slat, operated when the flaps extended, as directed by the US Navy.

Adequate stall warning was achieved with a rudder pedal shaker. The pitch changes associated with speed brake operation were satisfactorily reduced with an interconnect between the speed brake and the tailplane.

The first T45-A carried out its initial sea trials in December 1991. MDC

The first sea trials were conducted on the USS *John F Kennedy* in December 1991, after which the T-45A Goshawk was declared 'an operationally effective training aircraft' for the US Navy. Current US Navy plans call for the procurement of up to 174 T-45As, 32 flight simulators, four training integration system computers and 49 computer-assisted training devices in the multi-billion dollar T-45TS programme.
Customer: United States Navy (T-45A).

Technical Data
Length overall: 39ft 3in (11.97m);
Wing span: 30ft 10in (10.89m);
Wing area: 179.64sq ft (16.69sq m)
Height overall: 14ft 0in (4.27m);
Basic mass empty: 9,860lb (4,473kg)
Maximum take off weight: 14,500lb (6,577kg)
Maximum level speed: 550kt/0.83M
Maximum Mach number: Mach 1.04
Maximum load factors: -3g to +7.33g
Endurance: 3hr 10min.

Notes:
(1) Future production T-45A Goshawks, from aircraft No 73 onwards will feature 'Cockpit 21', a digital cockpit layout based around two monochrome multi-function displays (MFDs), a head-up display (HUD) and Global Positioning System (GPS) linked via a MIL-STD-1553B databus.

(2) A 'wet' intake modification, proposed from aircraft No 49 onwards, to increase range and endurance for certain missions, has been discontinued.

Hawk Mk 60 Series
Two-seat advanced flying and weapons training aircraft, with secondary ground-attack capability. Current export trainer version of the Hawk, developed from the earlier Mk 50 Series. First flown on 1 April 1982.

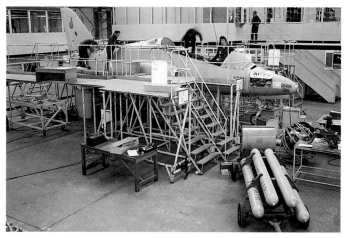

The Air Force of Zimbabwe was the initial customer for the Hawk 60 – the first aircraft on assembly at Dunsfold in 1981. BAe

Principal features of the Hawk Mk 60 Series:
• Uprated Rolls-Royce/Turboméca Adour Mk 861 turbofan engine (5,700lb st)
• Aerodynamically refined wing, with revised leading edge dressing and four-position flaps
• Higher rated wheels and tyres
• Can carry larger external fuel tanks of 130 Imp gal (590 litres) capacity, cleared to 8g.

Hawk 60 (for Zimbabwe) on a weapons trial flight in 1982. BAe

Aerodynamic revision to the Hawk 60 series wing has added three inboard mini-fences and a single breaker strip, to the larger outboard wing fence. Later wings have fixed leading

This Abu Dhabi Hawk 63 shows its mini wing fences, larger outboard wing fence and 130 gal external fuel tanks. BAe

edge droop (referred as the combat wing). The original three-position flaps (0°/25°/50°) of earlier variants, have also given way to four-position flaps, incorporating a setting of 12.5° for combat manoeuvring.

When compared to the basic Hawk T1, the Hawk 60 Series aircraft has:-

- Maximum operating weight increased 50%
- Maximum disposal load increased 125%
- Fuel load increased 69%
- Maximum ferry range increased 65%

More recent changes have included the adoption of an optional lengthened nose profile, similar to that incorporated on the Hawk 100. Hawk 60 Series aircraft, so equipped, cannot be retrospectively fitted with the forward looking infra-red (FLIR) and laser sensors of the Hawk 100 Series.

Abu Dhabi now operates two hybrid variants of the 60 Series – the Mk 63A and the Mk 63C – both of which are powered by Adour Mk 871 turbofan engines of 5,845lb st. In addition, these aircraft also feature the seven-station combat wing of the 100/200 Series, with combat manoeuvre flaps and provision for wingtip-mounted air-to-air missiles. A number of avionic refinements are also incorporated in the aircraft. The Mk 63C aircraft are new-build aircraft, while the Mk 63As are the original Mk 63 fuselages mated to the new combat wing.

Customers: Zimbabwe (Mk 60); UAE – Dubai (Mk 61); UAE – Abu Dhabi (Mk 63/63A/63C); Kuwait (Mk 64); Saudi Arabia (Mk 65); Switzerland (Mk 66) and Republic of Korea (Mk 67).

Technical Data
Length overall (short nose): 38ft 7in (11.80m);
Wing span: 30ft 10in (9.39m);
Wing area: 179.64 sq ft (16.69sq m)
Height overall: 13ft 2in (4.00m);
Basic mass empty: 8,845lb (4,012kg)
Maximum take off weight: 20,062lb (9,100kg)
Maximum level speed: 545kt/Mach 0.82
Maximum Mach number: Mach 1.2
Maximum load factors: +8g to -4g +6g to -3g (6,000lb weapons + 60% fuel).

Hawk 65 2110, the first of 30 delivered to Saudi Arabia from October 1987. BAe/GEOFF LEE

Hawk T66s at the Swiss Air Force flying school at Sion, where they replaced Vampire T55s. R-R/PETER HOLMAN

BAe's Hawk 100 demonstrator. BAe/RAY TROLL

Hawk 100 Series

Two-seat fighter and advanced weapons systems training aircraft. Began life as the Hawk EGA (Enhanced Ground Attack) in the early 1980s. The BAe demonstrator aircraft (G-HAWK/ZA101) was extensively modified to serve as the Hawk 100 prototype and was flown for the first time on 1 October 1987.

Principal features of the Hawk 100 Series:

- Lengthened nose profile with provision for FLIR and laser sensors
- Seven-station combat wing with combat manoeuvre flaps and provision for wingtip-mounted air-to-air missiles
- Revised tailfin with radar warning receiver (RWR) fairing
- Uprated Rolls-Royce/Turboméca Adour Mk 871 Turbofan engine (5,845lb st)
- Enhanced avionic systems operating through a MIL-STD-1553B databus
- Advanced cockpit layout with multi-function displays and hands-on-throttle-and-stick controls.

Hawk 100 Series aircraft provide a cost-effective solution to fighter lead-in training, navigator and weapons systems operator training, and can also perform combat missions comparable with those of more-complex front line combat aircraft, both in poor weather and by night.

Customers: UAE – Abu Dhabi (Mk 102); Oman (Mk 103); Malaysia (Mk 108) and Indonesia (Mk 109).

Technical Data

Length overall: 40ft 7in (12.43m);
Wing span: (with missiles): 32ft 7in (9.94m);
Wing area: 179.64sq ft (16.69sq m)
Height overall: 13ft 1ins (3.98m);
Basic mass empty: 9,700lb (4,400kg)
Maximum take off weight: 20,062lb (9,100kg)
Maximum level speed: 550kt/0.83M
Maximum Mach number: Mach 1.2
Maximum load factors: +8g to -4g
+6g to -3g (6,000lb Weapons + 60% fuel).

BAe demonstrator G-HAWK/ZA101 was modified as the Hawk 100 prototype in 1987. BAe

The Hawk 100 shows its longer nose, taller fin with RWR and seven-station combat wing with wing-tip missiles. BAe

Hawk 200 Series

Single-seat, radar-equipped, lightweight, multi-role combat aircraft. First aircraft, ZG200, made its maiden flight on 19 May 1986, but was lost on 2 July 1986. Replacement aircraft, ZH200 made its first flight on 2 April 1987.

The Hawk 200 features extensive structural and systems commonality with the 100 Series aircraft, aft of the rear cockpit bulkhead.

Principal features of the Hawk 200 Series:

• Revised forward fuselage with single-place cockpit
• New nose radome housing a Westinghouse APG-66H, multi-mode, pulse-Doppler radar
• Seven-station combat wing with combat manoeuvre flaps and provision for wingtip-mounted air-to-air missiles
• Uprated Rolls-Royce/Turboméca Adour Mk 871 Turbofan engine (5,845lb st)
• Advanced cockpit layout with MFDs and HOTAS controls
• Enhanced avionic systems operating through a MIL-STD 1553B databus

Customers: Oman (Mk 203); Malaysia (Mk 208) and Indonesia (Mk 209).

Technical Data

Length overall: 37ft 3in (11.35m);
Wing span: (with missiles): 32ft 7in (9.94m);
Wing area: 179.64sq ft (16.69sq m).
Height overall: 13ft 1in (3.98m);
Basic mass empty: 9,810lb (4,450kg)
Maximum take off weight: 20,062lb (9,100kg)
Maximum level speed: 550kt/0.83M
Maximum Mach number: Mach 1.2
Maximum load factors: +8g to -4g
+6g to -3g (6,000lb Weapons +60% fuel)
Radar: Westinghouse APG-66H multi-mode, pulse-Doppler. Operates in X-Band with ten air-to-air modes and four sub-modes for detection and tracking of airborne targets and a similar number for detection and tracking of ground-based and maritime targets.

The Hawk 200 Radar Development Aircraft, here carrying wing-tip AIM-9 Sidewinder missiles in its air defence fighter role. BAe

The second Hawk 200 equipped as a fighter-reconnaissance aircraft. BAe

The RAF ordered 176 Hawks, in March 1972, all of which had been delivered by 1982. BAe

APPENDIX B
ORDERS & DELIVERIES

Hawk orders, deliveries and operational status

TYPE	NUMBER ORDERED	DATE ORDERED	DATE DELIVERED	NUMBER IN SERVICE *
T1 (RAF)	176	Mar 1972	1976-1981	148
T1A (RAF)	(88)	Upgrade only	1983-1986	
Mk 50 (BAe Demo)	1	-	May 1976	-
Mk 51 (Finland)	50	29 Dec 1977	1980-1985	47
Mk 51A (Finland)	7	Dec 1990	1993	7
Mk 52 (Kenya)	12	Feb 1978	1980-1981	6
Mk 53 (Indonesia)	20	8 - Apr 1978 4 - May 1981 5 - Oct 1981 3 - Nov 1982	6 - 1980 2 - 1981 4 - 1982 5 - 1983 3 - 1984	14
T-45A (US Navy)	174	2 - 1985 12 - FY88 24 - FY88/9 12 Each - FY92 to FY95	1990-	52
Mk 60 (Zimbabwe)	8	Jan 1981	1982	6
Mk 60A (Zimbabwe)	5	Mar 1990	1992	5
Mk 61 (Dubai)	9	8 - Jun 1981 1 - Aug 1986	1983 1988	5
Mk 63 (Abu Dhabi)	16	Jan 1983	1984-1985	14
Mk 63A (Abu Dhabi)		Upgrade only	1992-	
Mk 63C (Abu Dhabi)	4	1992	Feb 1995	4
Mk 64 (Kuwait)	12	31 Oct 1983	1986	12
Mk 65 (Saudi Arabia)	30	Feb 1986	1987-1988	30
Mk 65A (Saudi Arabia)	20	Sep 1994	1996	-
Mk 66 (Switzerland)	20	Oct 1987	1989-1991	19
Mk 67 (Rep of Korea)	20	Dec 1989	1992-1993	17
Mk 102 (Abu Dhabi)	18	May 1989	1993-1994	18
Mk 103 (Oman)	4	Aug 1990	1993	4
Mk 108 (Malaysia)	10	Sep 1990	1993-1995	9
Mk 109 (Indonesia)	8	Jun 1993	1996	-
Mk 203 (Oman)	12	Aug 1990	1994-1995	12
Mk 208 (Malaysia)	18	Dec 1990	1994-1995	18
Mk 209 (Indonesia)	16	Jun 1993	1996	

Approximate number in service May 1995.

Finland was the first export customer for the Hawk. This Mk 51 HW-338 was delivered in August 1984, one of 50 ordered on 29 December 1977. BAe

Hawk 53 LL-5301 was the first of the 20 aircraft for Indonesia, delivered on 1 September 1980. BAe

Kenya was the second overseas customer for the Hawk, ordering 12 T52s in February 1978. BAe

Hawk Mk 60 (No 600) was the first of a batch of eight delivered to Zimbabwe in July 1982. BAe

One of 12 Hawk T64s delivered to Kuwait in 1986. BAe

Initially flown on 11 November 1982 this Hawk T61 was delivered to Dubai in March 1983, the first of eight ordered in June 1981.

Swiss Air Force Hawk T66s were manufactured jointly by BAe and Swiss industry, with assembly and test flying undertaken at the Swiss Federal Aircraft Factory at Emmen. F&W FOTO

The third of 20 Hawk Mk 67s ordered by the Republic of Korea in December 1989. BAe

Hawk T65 2118, that was delivered to Saudi Arabia on 11 January 1988, one of 30 ordered in February 1986. BAe

In 1992 Abu Dhabi ordered four new build Hawk Mk 63Cs, with the seven-station combat wing and an improved Adour Mk 871 engine. The second aircraft was delivered from Warton on 21 January 1995. BAe

Abu Dhabi ordered 18 Hawk 102s in May 1989 for delivery during 1993. BAe

The first of four Hawk 103s ordered in August 1990 and delivered on 7 December 1993 to Oman. BAe

Hawk 208s M40-32 and M40-38 taking off on their delivery flight to Malaysia in March 1995. BAe

APPENDIX C
OPERATORS WORLDWIDE

Abu Dhabi

The Abu Dhabi Air Force ordered its first Hawks - 16 Hawk Mk 63s - on 2 January 1983 and these were delivered in 1984 and 1985. Abu Dhabi subsequently ordered 18 Mk 102s in May 1989, being the launch customer for the Hawk 100 series and announced, at the same time, that it would upgrade its fleet of Mk 63s to Mk 63A standard. With Mk 63A aircraft, the existing Hawk Mk 63 fuselage is mated to a new, seven-station 'ᵒcombat' wing and an uprated Adour Mk 871 turbofan engine is installed. British Aerospace delivered the first two upgraded Mk 63As to Abu Dhabi on 3 February 1992 and the final aircraft will be handed over in 1995.

Only two Mk 63As were completely refurbished in the United Kingdom. Work on the remainder was split between British Aerospace - who manufactured the wings - and the Abu Dhabi Air Force, who undertook the avionic modifications and the installation of the new engine.

In 1992, Abu Dhabi ordered four new-build aircraft to Mk 63A standard - and these were subsequently designated as the Hawk Mk 63C. The first two Mk 63Cs were ferried from Warton in February 1995, with the two remaining aircraft delivered in April 1995. The last of the 18 Hawk Mk 102s was delivered on 23 December 1993.

Hawk 102s (1066 and 1068) were delivered to Abu Dhabi on 23 December 1993. BAe/GEOFF LEE

Dubai

The United Arab Emirates ordered eight Hawk T61s on 30 June 1981 for the Dubai Air Wing. They were delivered between March and September 1983. A further aircraft, as an attrition replacement, was ordered in August 1986 and delivered on 15 November 1988.

Hawk 61 501, the first of eight delivered to Dubai on 29 March 1983. A ninth aircraft was delivered in November 1988
BAe/PHIL HINDLEY

Finland

The Finnish Air Force, the *Ilmavoimat*, ordered 50 Hawk Mk 51s on 29 December 1977 to replace its Fouga Magisters for advanced flying and weapons training. They are also used by the Finnish Air Academy (*Ilmasotaikuolo*) and with the Special Reconnaissance Unit at Tikkakoski. It was chosen after keen international competition, in which the Hawk was up against the Alpha Jet, Saab 105, MB339 and L-39. One of the attractions of the Hawk was its tolerance to extreme climatic conditions, particularly the very low temperatures in which the Finnish Air Force has to operate.

The Finnish Hawks differ from the RAF Hawk T1s in having five weapons stations, instead of three. The Mk 51 features a Saab gunsight and is fitted with an indigenous VKT 12.7mm machine gun for training in the ground attack and air-to-air combat roles. They are also modified to accommodate Vinten reconnaissance pods, which can be fitted with conventional reconnaissance cameras and infra-red linescan sensors.

HW-355, one of seven Hawk 51As that were assembled in the UK, and delivered to the Finnish Air Force in 1993/94. BAe

This Hawk Mk 51 replaced a Fouga Magister at the Finnish Air Academy. BAe

Hawk Mk 53, one of 20 delivered to Indonesia between 1978 and 1982. BAe

The first four aircraft were produced in the United Kingdom and the first two of these were delivered to Finland in December 1980. The remaining 46 aircraft were assembled by Valmet in Finland, using components produced in the United Kingdom and in Finland. Deliveries from Valmet commenced early in 1981 and was completed by October 1985.

Finland subsequently ordered seven Hawk Mk 51As, all of which were assembled in the United Kingdom, and delivered between 1993 and 1994.

Indonesia

Indonesia ordered 20 Hawk Mk 53s, in four batches, between April 1978 and November 1982 and the aircraft were delivered to the country over a five-year period from 1980 to 1984. The majority of the Hawk Mk 53s were delivered in camouflage, but the final three aircraft sported a red and white training colour scheme.

In June 1993, Indonesia confirmed its satisfaction with the Hawk, as an operational aircraft, by placing a follow-on order for eight two-seat Mk 109s and 16 single-seat Mk 209s. These will be delivered from 1996 onwards.

The final Hawk 53s delivered to Indonesia had the red and white training colour scheme of the Indonesian Air Force Flying Training School. LL-5318 was delivered on 7 February 1984. BAe

Artists impression of the Hawk 109, of which eight were ordered for the Indonesian Air Force in June 1993, along with 16 single-seat Hawk 209s. Deliveries of these aircraft will commence in 1996. BAe

Kenya

For many years British Aerospace was prevented, by a confidentially clause, from publicising the fact that the Kenyan Air Force had ordered 12 Hawk Mk 52s on 9 February 1978 to replace its BAC Strikemasters. The company was subject to the political sensitivity associated with arms trading with African states. As a result BAe was not permitted to release for publication, photographs of any Hawks in Kenyan colours and markings. The Hawk 52 was the first version to be fitted with a braking parachute, a feature deemed necessary for operation from the African country's `hot and high' airfields. The aircraft were delivered in 1980 and 1981.

Four of the 12 Hawk 52s supplied to the Kenyan Air Force in 1981/82. BAe

Republic of Korea (South Korea)

The Republic of Korea Air Force is, to date, the sole operator of the long nose version of the Hawk Mk 60. Twenty Hawk Mk 67s were ordered in December 1989 and delivered between June 1992 and August 1993.

ROKAF Hawk 67, 67-503 landing at Warton at the end of a test flight, prior to delivery in early 1993. To date, South Korea is the only country to opt for the long nose 60 series Hawk. BOB ARCHER

No 145, one of six Kuwait Air Force Hawk 64s that were seized by Iraq in 1990, and subsequently recaptured and returned to service. BAe

Kuwait

The Kuwait Air Force ordered 12 Hawk Mk 64s on 31 October 1983, all of which were delivered in 1986. During the Iraqi invasion of Kuwait in August 1990, six aircraft were liberated to Sharjah, but the remaining six fell to the Iraqis and were taken across the border by the invaders. These Hawks were subsequently recovered, having suffered varying degrees of damage. They were all subsequently returned to flight status, with the help of British Aerospace.

Malaysia

In December 1990, the Royal Malaysian Air Force placed an order for ten Hawk Mk 108s and 18 Hawk Mk 208s, becoming the second customer for the Hawk 200. Deliveries began in February 1994 and will be completed in 1995. RMAF Hawks incorporate nosewheel steering and the Mk 208s have a fixed in-flight refuelling probe level with the starboard side of the windscreen.

Roll-out of Malaysian Air Force Hawk 108 MT003/M40-03 at Warton in January 1994. BAe/RAY TROLL

Hawk 208 M40-32 is shown here on a test flight from Warton, carrying a TAXAN towed target pod on the fuselage centreline pylon. It was delivered to Malaysia in March 1995. BAe/CHRIS RYDING

Oman

A long-established operator of British-built military aircraft the Royal Air Force of Oman ordered four Hawk Mk 103s and 12 Hawk Mk 203s on 30 July 1990, to replace its ageing Hunters. Oman was the launch customer for the Hawk 200 attack/interceptor variant. Deliveries of the Hawk Mk 103s began in December 1993 and the Hawk Mk 203s in October 1994. The final pair of Hawk Mk 203s were delivered in April 1995. It is likely that the single-seaters will be fitted with a refuelling probe once the RAF of Oman obtains a Hercules tanker.

One of the 12 Hawk 203s ordered by the Royal Air Force of Oman in July 1990 as a Hunter replacement, departing Warton in February 1995 on delivery. TERRY SENIOR

Saudi Arabia

As part of Phase 1 of the multi-billion pound Al Yamamah Project, the Royal Saudi Air Force ordered 30 Hawk T65s in February 1986. These aircraft were delivered to Saudi Arabia between October 1987 and October 1988. With the announcement of Phase II of the Al Yamamah Project, the Royal Saudi Air Force confirmed an order for an additional 20 Hawk T65As in September 1994, for delivery from 1996.

Royal Saudi Air Force Hawk Mk 65, armed with AIM-9L sidewinder missiles and a 30mm Aden gun pod, for air defence duties during the Gulf War. IAN BLACK

Switzerland

On 20 October 1987, the Swiss Air Force *Flugwaffe* ordered 20 Hawk T66s to replace its elderly Vampire T55 advanced jet trainers. The first aircraft U-1251 was assembled in the United Kingdom, whilst the remaining 19 aircraft were assembled from kits by the Swiss Federal Aircraft Factory at Emmen. The first UK-built Hawk T66 was flown to Switzerland in November 1989 and all 20 aircraft were operational by the end of 1991.

The first Swiss Air Force Hawk T66 (U-1251) heads a colourful line of 18 trainers at Sion. R-R/PETER HOLMAN

Four different colours for RAF Hawk operators, photographed in 1984. Top to bottom: *TIA Red Arrows; TIA No 1 TWU/234 (Reserve) Squadron; TIA No 1 TWU/79 (Reserve) Squadron; TI No 4 FTS.* BAe

United Kingdom

The Ministry of Defence ordered 176 Hawk T1s, the first (XX162 and XX163) being delivered on 4 November 1976, with the last (XX353) leaving the factory on 9 February 1982. The sixth pre-production aircraft (XX160) was the last to enter service with the RAF on 16 May 1982. Hawks have mainly equipped No 4 FTS and CFS (Valley), the former No 1 TWU (Brawdy) and No 2 TWU/7 FTS (Chivenor). In 1995 some 150 Hawk T1/T1As remain in service as follows: No 4 FTS (66), No 6 FTS (10), No 100 Sqn (16), *Red Arrows* (12), ETPS and other MoD(PE) units (12); the RN Fleet Requirements and Direction Unit (FRADU) at RNAS Yeovilton has 16; a further 16 are stored at RAF Shawbury and two are operated by RAF St Athan Station Flight.

There is no mistaking where these Hawk T1As were based. BAe

United States

On 18 November 1981 the United States Navy announced the selection of a training system based on a derivative of the Hawk as the winner of its prestigious VTXTS competition, to find a new carrier-capable advanced jet trainer to replace its existing fleet of T-2C Buckeye and TA-4J Skyhawk trainers. Designated T-45A Goshawk, this navalised development of the Hawk T1/50 entered US Navy service on 23 January 1992, over two years later than planned, owing to shortcomings with the US Navy's originally-specified design.

The US Navy **hopes** eventually to acquire up to 218 T-45A Goshawks, as part of its multi-billion dollar T-45TS jet pilot training system.

Zimbabwe

The Air Force of Zimbabwe ordered eight Hawk Mk 60s in January 1981 and the first four of these were delivered to No 2 Squadron, at Thornhill Air Base, on 15 July 1982. On Sunday, 25 July 1982, all four aircraft had explosive charges thrown down their intakes by political insurgents. One Hawk was destroyed, another was slightly damaged and repaired in-country, and two others were air freighted back to the United Kingdom for major repair by British Aerospace. Zimbabwe subsequently ordered five additional Hawk Mk 60As in March 1990, all of which were delivered in 1992.

T-45A Goshawks started to replace T-2C Buckeyes and TA-4J Skyhawks for US Navy pilot training at Kingsville, Texas from early 1992.

Zimbabwe Hawk 60 603 was badly damaged by terrorist action within a week of arriving in the country in July 1982. It was subsequently rebuilt by British Aerospace. BAe

Zimbabwe Hawk 60 603 back in action after its repair. R-R/PETER HOLMAN

APPENDIX D
HAWK PRODUCTION LIST

W/N	MARK	SERIAL	FIRST FLT	DELIVERY	COMMENTS
312001	T1	XX154	21.08.74	18.01.82	
312002	T1	XX156		18.11.77	
312003	T1A	XX157		19.12.79	
312004	T1A	XX158		17.03.82	
312005	T1A	XX159		05.01.79	
312006	T1	XX160		16.05.82	
312007	T1	XX161	04.76	22.12.76	
312009	T1	XX162		04.11.76	
312010	T1	XX163		04.11.76	Cr 01.07.93 Valley - turned back after take-off
312011	T1	XX164		01.12.76	
312012	T1	XX165		06.12.76	
312013	T1	XX166		30.12.76	Cr 24.06.83 North Barrule IOM
312014	T1	XX167		31.01.77	
312015	T1	XX168		04.04.77	G-9-543 (19.04.85 - 24.04.85)
312016	T1	XX169		21.01.77	
312017	T1	XX170		03.03.77	
312018	T1	XX171		04.04.77	
312019	T1	XX172		29.04.77	
312020	T1	XX173		19.05.77	
312021	T1	XX174		03.05.77	
312022	T1	XX175		16.06.77	
312023	T1	XX176		14.06.77	
312024	T1	XX177		01.08.77	
312025	T1	XX178		22.08.77	
312026	T1	XX179		02.09.77	
312027	T1	XX180		03.10.77	Cr 07.11.84 Mona - birdstrike
312028	T1	XX181		13.09.77	
312029	T1	XX182		04.11.77	Cr 14.06.89 mid-Wales - collided with XX291
312030	T1	XX183		07.11.77	
312031	T1	XX184		15.11.77	
312032	T1	XX185		21.11.77	
312033	T1A	XX186		12.01.78	
312034	T1A	XX187		02.12.77	
312035	T1A	XX188		20.01.78	
312036	T1A	XX189		23.02.78	
312037	T1A	XX190		02.12.77	

The first Hawk T1 was displayed at Farnborough soon after its maiden flight on 21 August 1974. PETER R MARCH

XX156 was delivered to the RAF on 18 November 1977.
BRIAN STRICKLAND

Development Hawk XX158 was the last Hawk to be delivered to the RAF – on 17 March 1982. PETER R MARCH

The fifth pre-production Hawk XX159 was specially painted for the Brawdy solo display pilot in 1987. BAe

1992 Valley display Hawk T1 XX163 crashed at its home base while taking off for a training flight on 1 July 1993. PETER R MARCH

Large tiger's head of No 74(R) Sqn adorns the tail of black Hawk T1 XX226, flying with No 4 FTS. RAF VALLEY

W/N	MARK	SERIAL	FIRST FLT	DELIVERY	COMMENTS
312038	T1A	XX191		06.01.78	
312039	T1A	XX192		02.03.78	Cr 20.09.89 Brawdy
312040	T1A	XX193		23.03.78	
312041	T1A	XX194		24.02.78	
312042	T1	XX195		03.04.78	
312043	T1A	XX196		14.03.78	
312044	T1A	XX197		03.04.78	Cr 13.05.88 - loss of power on take off
312045	T1A	XX198		03.04.78	
312046	T1A	XX199		06.02.78	
312047	T1A	XX200		02.03.78	
312048	T1A	XX201		27.04.78	
312049	T1A	XX202		02.05.78	
312050	T1A	XX203		30.03.78	
312051	T1A	XX204		10.05.78	
312052	T1A	XX205		30.06.78	
312053	T1A	XX217		18.05.78	
312054	T1A	XX218		28.04.78	
312055	T1A	XX219		05.07.78	
312056	T1A	XX220		10.05.78	
312057	T1A	XX221		30.06.78	
312058	T1A	XX222		30.06.78	
312059	T1	XX223		05.06.78	Cr 07.07.86 - left runway Valley, tore off u/c
312060	T1	XX224		03.07.78	
312061	T1	XX225		12.07.78	
312062	T1	XX226		27.07.78	
312063	T1A	XX227		14.07.78	RA
312064	T1	XX228		02.08.78	
312065	T1	XX229		23.08.78	Cr 29.07.83 - engine failure 50m SW of Brawdy
312066	T1A	XX230		07.08.78	
312067	T1W	XX231		01.09.78	
312068	T1	XX232		02.10.78	
312069	T1	XX233		12.09.78	RA
312070	T1	XX234		22.09.78	
312071	T1	XX235		18.10.78	
312072	T1	XX236		26.09.78	
312073	T1	XX237		31.10.78	RA
312074	T1	XX238		07.10.81	
312075	T1	XX239		27.09.78	

1992 Strike Command display Hawk T1A XX230 was from No2 TWU/63 Sqn at RAF Chivenor. BAe

Hawk T1 XX238 specially painted for the CFS, Support Command solo display pilot in 1987. BAe

W/N	MARK	SERIAL	FIRST FLT	DELIVERY	COMMENTS
312076	T1	XX240		27.10.78	
312077	T1	XX241		01.11.78	RA Cr 16.11.87 - collided with XX259 over Welton
312078	T1	XX242		02.11.78	
312079	T1A	XX243		21.11.78	RA Cr 22.01.88 - loss of control
312080	T1	XX244		29.11.78	
312081	T1	XX245		04.12.78	
312082	T1A	XX246		29.11.78	
312083	T1A	XX247		13.11.78	
312084	T1A	XX248		18.12.78	
312085	T1	XX249		21.12.78	
312086	T1	XX250		04.12.78	
312087	T1	XX251		15.12.78	RA Cr 21.03.84 Akrotiri - struck ground
312088	T1A	XX252		03.01.79	RA
312089	T1A	XX253		18.12.78	RA
312090	T1A	XX254		15.11.78	
312091	T1A	XX255		05.01.79	
312092	T1A	XX256		19.12.78	
312093	T1	XX257		02.02.79	RA Cr 31.08.84 Sidmouth - LP2 failure
312094	T1A	XX258	19.04.79	06.06.79	
312095	T1	XX259		03.01.79	RA Cr 16.11.87 - collided with XX241 over Welton
312096	T1A	XX260		22.02.79	RA
312097	T1A	XX261		03.01.79	
312098	T1	XX262		01.03.79	RA Cr 17.05.80 Brighton - hit yacht mast
312099	T1A	XX263		11.04.79	
312100	T1A	XX264		13.03.79	RA
312101	T1A	XX265		27.03.79	
312102	T1A	XX266		22.03.79	RA
312103	T1A	XX278		03.01.79	

1991 display Hawk T1 XX249 in special markings to mark the 70th anniversary of 4 FTS '1921 Abu Sueir – Valley 1991', in formation with No 25 Sqn's Tornado F3. BAe

The RAF's Red Arrows aerobatic team has been flying the Hawk for over 15 years, losing eight aircraft in accidents during that time.
PETER R MARCH

W/N	MARK	SERIAL	FIRST FLT	DELIVERY	COMMENTS
312104	T1A	XX279		20.04.79	Cr 30.01.85 - loss of control
312105	T1A	XX280		01.05.79	
312106	T1A	XX281		05.06.79	
312107	T1A	XX282		29.06.79	
312108	T1	XX283	19.06.79	10.07.79	
312109	T1A	XX284		20.07.79	
312110	T1A	XX285		23.05.79	
312111	T1A	XX286		20.07.79	
312112	T1A	XX287		21.09.79	
312113	T1W	XX288		05.09.79	
312114	T1A	XX289		12.10.79	
312115	T1	XX290		12.10.79	
312116	T1	XX291		29.11.79	Cr 14.06.89 Mid Wales - collided with XX182
312117	T1W	XX292		02.11.79	
312118	T1	XX293		18.12.79	Cr 17.04.85 Wattisham - lost canopy
312119	T1	XX294		13.11.79	RA
312120	T1	XX295		28.11.79	
312121	T1	XX296		20.12.79	
312122	T1A	XX297		02.02.80	RA Cr 03.11.86 Scampton - engine surge flameout
312123	T1	XX298		11.12.79	Cr 25.10 84 - control restriction, off Llanbedr
312124	T1W	XX299		04.01.80	
312125	T1	XX300		22.01.80	Cr 20.10.82 - bird strike, Chivenor
312126	T1A	XX301		13.02.80	
312127	T1A	XX302		08.01.80	
312128	T1A	XX303		16.01.80	
312129	T1A	XX304		07.03.80	RA Cr 24.06.88 - on take-off
312130	T1	XX305		01.02.80	Cr 28.07.82, Valley
312131	T1A	XX306		29.02.80	RA
312132	T1	XX307		29.02.80	RA
312133	T1	XX308		23.04.80	RA
312134	T1	XX309		31.03.80	
312135	T1W	XX310		30.04.80	
312136	T1	XX311		29.04.80	
312137	T1	XX312		02.06.80	
312138	T1	XX313		03.07.80	
312139	T1	XX314		31.07.80	
312140	T1A	XX315		28.07.80	
312141	T1A	XX316		27.08.80	

Hawk T1W XX299 in grey/green camouflage, took part in the air-to-air visibility trials at RAF Chivenor in November 1992.

Hawk T1 XX314 wearing No 151 Squadron colours operating with No 2 TWU at Chivenor. PETER R MARCH

XX283, a Hawk T1, was first flown on 19 June 1979 and delivered to the RAF the following month. In 1993 it was one of the first Hawks operated by No 100 Squadron. PETER R MARCH

Hawk T1As XX289 and XX157 respectively in the colours of No 7 FTS 19 (R) Squadron and No 92 (R) Squadron flying over RAF Chivenor.

On a misty morning, XX314, now painted black with No 4 FTS, stands out well. BAe/GEOFF LEE

W/N	MARK	SERIAL	FIRST FLT	DELIVERY	COMMENTS
312142	T1A	XX317		29.09.80	
312143	T1A	XX318		24.09.80	
312144	T1A	XX319		15.10.80	
312145	T1A	XX320		24.11.80	
312146	T1A	XX321		24.11.80	
312147	T1A	XX322		24.11.80	
312148	T1A	XX323		01.12.80	
312149	T1A	XX324		01.12.80	
312150	T1	XX325		04.12.80	
312151	T1A	XX326		16.12.80	
312152	T1	XX327		04.12.80	
312153	T1A	XX329		18.12.80	
312154	T1A	XX330		05.01.81	
312155	T1A	XX331		18.12.80	
312156	T1A	XX332		05.01.81	
312157	T1A	XX333		05.01.81	Cr 26.09.85, Decimomannu - collided with XX340
312158	T1A	XX334		06.01.81	Cr 30.09.92, Chivenor - turn back
312159	T1A	XX335		06.01.81	
312160	T1	XX336		08.01.81	Cr 29.07.83 - collided with XX353, Taw Estuary
312161	T1A	XX337		02.03.81	
312162	T1W	XX338		07.10.81	
312163	T1	XX339		16.08.82	
312164	T1A	XX340		05.05.81	Cr 26.09.85, Decimomannu - collided with XX333
312165	T1	XX341		13.05.81	ASTRA modified
312166	T1	XX342		05.06.81	
312167	T1	XX343		03.07.81	
312168	T1	XX344		22.07.81	Cr 07.01.82, Bedford
312169	T1A	XX345		30.09.81	
312170	T1A	XX346		13.10.81	
312171	T1	XX347		06.11.81	Cr 09.05.90 - control loss
312172	T1A	XX348		27.10.81	
312173	T1W	XX349		16.11.81	
312174	T1A	XX350		19.11.81	
312175	T1A	XX351		18.01.82	
312176	T1A	XX352		20.01.82	
312177	T1	XX353		09.02.82	Cr 29.07.83 - collided with XX336, nr Holsworthy
312008	50	G-HAWK /ZA101	17.05.76		ff 20.08.86 (60 Srs); ff 01.10.87 (100 Srs)

XX323 Hawk T1A operating with No 1 TWU/234 Sqn at RAF Brawdy in 1986. BAe

Above
Hawk operators in 1990 –
TIA XX324 234 Sqn/1TWU, Brawdy
TIA XX322 151 Sqn/2TWU, Chivenor
T1 XX164 4FTS, Valley and
T1A XX260 Red Arrows, Scampton.
BAe

Left
Hawk T1 XX347 was lost in an
accident on 9 May 1990. BAe

W/N	MARK	LINE NO	SERIAL	FIRST FLT	DELIVERY	REGIST'N	UK SERIAL	CUSTOMER	COMMENTS
312178	52	107	1001	03.12.79	11.04.80	G-9-454	ZB609	Kenya	Cr 11.03.88
312179	52	117	1002		11.04.80	G-9-455		Kenya	
312180	52	120	1003		11.04.80	G-9-456		Kenya	Cr 26.02.82 Nr Nanyuki
312181	52	123	1004		28.05.80	G-9-457		Kenya	
312182	52	128	1005		28.05.80	G-9-458		Kenya	
312183	52	130	1006		29.07.80	G-9-459		Kenya	
312184	52	136	1007		29.07.80	G-9-460		Kenya	
312185	52	140	1008		28.08.80	G-9-461		Kenya	
312186	52	146	1009		28.08.80	G-9-462		Kenya	Cr 11.11.88
312187	52	151	1010		06.02.81	G-9-463		Kenya	
312188	52	154	1011		06.02.81	G-9-464		Kenya	
312189	52	157	1012		06.02.81	G-9-465		Kenya	
312190	53	126	LL-5301	06.06.80	01.09.80	G-9-466	ZB618	Indonesia	
312191	53	152	LL-5302		01.09.80	G-9-467		Indonesia	Cr 17.09.81 aerobatics
312192	53	155	LL-5303		17.09.80	G-9-468		Indonesia	Cr 10.08.83
312193	53	161	LL-5304		17.09.80	G-9-469		Indonesia	Cr 22.10.81
312194	53	166	LL-5305		19.11.80	G-9-470		Indonesia	
312195	53	171	LL-5306		19.11.80	G-9-471		Indonesia	
312196	53	175	LL-5307		06.01.81	G-9-472		Indonesia	Cr 17.06.81 collision
312197	53	179	LL-5308		06.01.81	G-9-473		Indonesia	Cr 17.06.81 collision
312256	53	222	LL-5309	02.07.82	10.08.82	G-9-494		Indonesia	
312257	53	223	LL-5310	14.07.82	10.08.82	G-9-495		Indonesia	
312258	53	226	LL-5311	02.09.82	19.10.82	G-9-496		Indonesia	
312259	53	227	LL-5312	23.09.82	19.10.82	G-9-497		Indonesia	
312260	53	228	LL-5313		15.03.83	G-9-498		Indonesia	
312268	53	244	LL-5314	15.02.83	15.03.83	G-9-499		Indonesia	
312269	53	245	LL-5315	09.03.83	14.06.83	G-9-500		Indonesia	
312270	53	246	LL-5316	31.03.83	14.06.83	G-9-501		Indonesia	
312271	53	249	LL-5317	05.05.83	14.06.83	G-9-510		Indonesia	
312279	53	253	LL-5318	29.11.83	07.02.84	G-9-511		Indonesia	Cr 20.06.89
312278	53	254	LL-5319	06.01.84	06.03.84	G-9-512		Indonesia	
312279	53	255	LL-5320	10.02.84	06.03.84	G-9-513		Indonesia	

The first Hawk 52s for the Kenyan Air Force (1001-1003) departing Dunsfold on delivery 11 April 1980. BAe

Indonesian Hawk 53 LL-5304, delivered on 17 September 1980, but was written off on 22 October 1981. BAe

W/N	MARK	LINE NO	SERIAL	FIRST FLT	DELIVERY	REGIST'N	UK SERIAL	CUSTOMER	COMMENTS
312248	60	209	600	01.04.82	13.07.82	G-9-486		Zimbabwe	Bomb damage
		Rebuild	600	07.08.84	17.10.84			Zimbabwe	
312249	60	210	601	20.04.82	13.07.82	G-9-487		Zimbabwe	
312250	60	211	602	12.05.82	13.07.82	G-9-488		Zimbabwe	Destroyed 25.07.82
312251	60	212	603	07.06.82	13.07.82	G-9-489		Zimbabwe	Bomb damage
		Rebuild	603	18.09.84	17.10.84			Zimbabwe	
312252	60	213	604	09.08.82	05.10.82	G-9-490		Zimbabwe	
312253	60	219	605	27.08.82	05.10.82	G-9-491		Zimbabwe	
312254	60	220	606	16.09.82	05.10.82	G-9-492		Zimbabwe	
312255	60	221	607	22.09.82	05.10.82	G-9-493		Zimbabwe	
312198	51	133	HW-301	21.01.81	20.02.81			Finland	By road & sea 07.80
312199	51	153	HW-302	16.10.80	16.12.80	G-9-474	ZB622	Finland	Cr 17.03.81
312200	51	173	HW-303	10.80	19.12.80	G-9-475		Finland	
312201	51	181	HW-304	19.01.81	20.02.81			Finland	By road & sea 12.80
312202	51	184	HW-305		23.06.81	G-9-476	ZD226	Finland	
312203	51	200	HW-306		23.06.81	G-9-477		Finland	
312204	51	204	HW-307		18.09.81			Finland	
312205	51	205	HW-308		10.11.81			Finland	
312206	51	206	HW-309		09.12.81			Finland	
312207	51	207	HW-310		15.01.82			Finland	
312208	51	208	HW-311		19.03.82			Finland	
312209	51	214	HW-312		29.03.82			Finland	
312210	51	215	HW-313		26.04.82			Finland	Cr 09.05.86
312211	51	216	HW-314		19.05.82			Finland	
312212	51	217	HW-315		21.06.82			Finland	
312213	51	218	HW-316		09.08.82			Finland	
312214	51	224	HW-317		24.09.82			Finland	Cr 05.12.89
312215	51	225	HW-318		27.10.82			Finland	
312216	51	229	HW-319		10.12.82			Finland	
312217	51	230	HW-320		06.01.83			Finland	
312218	51	231	HW-321		02.02.83			Finland	

Hawk 51 HW-338 has been in service with the Finnish Air Force since August 1984. BAe

W/N	MARK	LINE NO	SERIAL	FIRST FLT	DELIVERY	REGIST'N	UK SERIAL	CUSTOMER	COMMENTS
312219	51	235	HW-322	22.04.83	08.06.83			Finland	
312220	51	236	HW-323		28.04.83			Finland	
312221	51	237	HW-324		11.05.83			Finland	
312222	51	238	HW-325		26.05.83			Finland	
312223	51	239	HW-326		29.06.83			Finland	
312224	51	264	HW-327		14.09.83			Finland	
312225	51	265	HW-328		25.10.83			Finland	
312226	51	268	HW-329		30.12.83			Finland	
312227	51	272	HW-330		18.11.83			Finland	
312228	51	273	HW-331		17.01.84			Finland	
312229	51	274	HW-332		21.02.84			Finland	
312230	51	275	HW-333		13.03.84			Finland	
312231	51	276	HW-334		04.05.84			Finland	
312232	51	277	HW-335		13.04.84			Finland	
312233	51	278	HW-336		07.06.84			Finland	
312234	51	281	HW-337		06.07.84			Finland	
312235	51	282	HW-338		27.08.84			Finland	
312236	51	283	HW-339		10.10.84			Finland	
312237	51	285	HW-340		28.11.84			Finland	
312238	51	286	HW-341		09.01.85			Finland	
312239	51	288	HW-342		19.02.85			Finland	
312240	51	290	HW-343		22.03.85			Finland	
312241	51	247	HW-344		25.04.85			Finland	
312242	51	257	HW-345		28.05.85			Finland	
312243	51	294	HW-346		30.05.85			Finland	
312244	51	297	HW-347		05.07.85			Finland	
312245	51	300	HW-348		16.08.85			Finland	
312246	51	301	HW-349		12.09.85			Finland	
312247	51	302	HW-350	01.09.85	08.10.85			Finland	
312261	T61	232	501	11.11.82	29.03.83	G-9-502		UAE Dubai	
312262	T61	233	502	23.12.82	29.03.83	G-9-503		UAE Dubai	
312263	T61	234	503	16.02.83	29.03.83	G-9-504		UAE Dubai	Cr 04.09.90
312264	T61	240	504	13.04.83	07.06.83	G-9-505		UAE Dubai	Cr
312273	T61	248	505	13.05.83	07.06.83	G-9-506		UAE Dubai	Cr 04.04.86
312274	T61	250	506	17.06.83	06.09.83	G-9-507		UAE Dubai	Cr 18.12.91
312275	T61	251	507	20.07.83	06.09.83	G-9-508		UAE Dubai	Cr 25.04.94
312276	T61	252	508	05.08.83	06.09.83	G-9-509		UAE Dubai	
312265	63	241	1001	26.06.84	05.10.84	G-9-515		UAE Abu Dhabi	Upg'd to Mk 63A
312285	63	261	1002	11.07.84	05.10.84	G-9-516		UAE Abu Dhabi	Upg'd to Mk 63A
312286	63	262	1003	11.09.84	05.10.84	G-9-517		UAE Abu Dhabi	Cr 15.04.89
312287	63	263	1004	16.08.84	05.10.84	G-9-518		UAE Abu Dhabi	Upg'd to Mk 63A
312288	63	266	1005	07.08.84	08.12.84	G-9-519		UAE Abu Dhabi	Upg'd to Mk 63A
312289	63	267	1006	09.10.84	08.12.84	G-9-520		UAE Abu Dhabi	Upg'd to Mk 63A
312290	63	269	1007		08.12.84	G-9-521		UAE Abu Dhabi	Upg'd to Mk 63A
312291	63	270	1008		08.12.84	G-9-522		UAE Abu Dhabi	Upg'd to Mk 63A
312292	63	242	1009	28.11.84	04.01.85	G-9-523		UAE Abu Dhabi	Upg'd to Mk 63A
312293	63	243	1010	30.11.84	04.01.85	G-9-524		UAE Abu Dhabi	Upg'd to Mk 63A
312294	63	260	1011	23.01.85	29.03.85	G-9-525		UAE Abu Dhabi	Upg'd to Mk 63A
312295	63	256	1012	13.01.85	27.03.85	G-9-526		UAE Abu Dhabi	Upg'd to Mk 63A
312296	63	258	1013	27.01.85	29.03.85	G-9-527		UAE Abu Dhabi	Upg'd to Mk 63A
312297	63	259	1014	11.03.85	24.05.85	G-9-528	ZE472	UAE Abu Dhabi	Upg'd to Mk 63A
312298	63	291	1015	27.03.85	24.05.85	G-9-529		UAE Abu Dhabi	Upg'd to Mk 63A
312299	63	295	1016	04.04.85	24.05.85	G-9-530		UAE Abu Dhabi	Cr 24.02.87

W/N	MARK	LINE NO	SERIAL	FIRST FLT	DELIVERY	REGIST'N	UK SERIAL	CUSTOMER	COMMENTS
312267	64	279	140	16.09.85	04.10.85	G-9-531	ZF107	Kuwait	
312272	64	292	141	04.09.85	04.10.85	G-9-532		Kuwait	
312284	64	280	142	04.10.85	20.01.86	G-9-533	ZF108	Kuwait	
312280	64	284	143	25.10.85	20.01.86	G-9-534		Kuwait	
312282	64	287	144	19.11.85	11.03.86	G-9-535		Kuwait	
312283	64	289	145	12.12.85	11.03.86	G-9-536		Kuwait	
312300	64	296	146	24.01.86	11.03.86	G-9-537		Kuwait	
312302	64	299	147	12.02.86	03.06.86	G-9-538	ZF627	Kuwait	For Swiss trials
312303	64	303	148	03.04.86	03.06.86	G-9-539		Kuwait	
312304	64	304	149	08.05.86	03.06.86	G-9-540		Kuwait	
312306	64	306	150	25.06.86	23.09.86	G-9-541		Kuwait	
312266	64	271	151	20.08.86	23.09.86	G-9-542		Kuwait	
	200	SS1	ZG200	19.05.86				BAe	Cr 02.07.86, Alfold, Surrey
	T65	SA001	2110	26.06.87	12.10.87			Saudi Arabia	
	T65	SA002	2111	09.07.87	12.10.87			Saudi Arabia	
	T65	SA003	2112	29.07.87	01.09.87			Saudi Arabia	
	T65	SA004	2113	14.08.87	14.09.87			Saudi Arabia	
	T65	SA005	2114	03.09.87	26.10.87			Saudi Arabia	
	T65	SA006	2115	15.09.87	26.10.87			Saudi Arabia	
	T65	SA007	2116		25.01.88			Saudi Arabia	
	T65	SA008	2117		25.01.88			Saudi Arabia	
	T65	SA009	2118		11.01.88			Saudi Arabia	
	T65	SA010	2119		11.01.88			Saudi Arabia	
	T65	SA011	2120		25.01.88			Saudi Arabia	
	T65	SA012	2121		25.01.88			Saudi Arabia	
	T65	SA013	3751		26.02.88			Saudi Arabia	
	T65	SA014	3752		26.02.88			Saudi Arabia	
	T65	SA015	3753		28.03.88			Saudi Arabia	
	T65	SA016	3754		28.03.88			Saudi Arabia	
	T65	SA017	3755		25.04.88			Saudi Arabia	
	T65	SA018	3756		25.04.88			Saudi Arabia	

Hawk 64 145 was delivered to the Kuwait Air Force on 11 March 1986. BAe

Royal Saudi Air Force Hawk T65s (2111 to 2115) lined up in their sun shelters. BAe

Pre-flight inspection for Air Force of Zimbabwe Hawk T60A (609) R-R/PETER HOLMAN

W/N	MARK	LINE NO	SERIAL	FIRST FLT	DELIVERY	REGIST'N	UK SERIAL	CUSTOMER	COMMENTS
	T65	SA019	3757	05.05.88	23.05.88			Saudi Arabia	
	T65	SA020	3758	27.04.88	23.05.88			Saudi Arabia	
	T65	SA021	3759	26.05.88	26.06.88			Saudi Arabia	
	T65	SA022	3760	25.05.88	26.06.88			Saudi Arabia	
	T65	SA023	3761		25.10.88			Saudi Arabia	
	T65	SA024	3762		25.08.88			Saudi Arabia	
	T65	SA025	3763		25.08.88			Saudi Arabia	
	T65	SA026	3764		25.08.88			Saudi Arabia	
	T65	SA027	3765		26.09.88			Saudi Arabia	
	T65	SA028	3766		26.09.88			Saudi Arabia	
	T65	SA029	3767		25.10.88			Saudi Arabia	
	T65	SA030	3768		25.10.88			Saudi Arabia	
	T61	332	509		15.11.88			UAE Dubai	
	T66	SW001	U-1251	07.04.89	30.01.90		ZG974	Switzerland	
	T66	SW002	U-1252	19.12.89	06.03.90			Switzerland	
	T66	SW003	U-1253		29.03.90			Switzerland	
	T66	SW004	U-1254		22.05.90			Switzerland	
	T66	SW005	U-1255		23.05.90			Switzerland	
	T66	SW006	U-1256		19.06.90			Switzerland	Cr 15.10.90
	T66	SW007	U-1257		06.07.90			Switzerland	
	T66	SW008	U-1258		16.08.90			Switzerland	
	T66	SW009	U-1259		07.09.90			Switzerland	
	T66	SW010	U-1260		09.10.90			Switzerland	
	T66	SW011	U-1261		12.10.90			Switzerland	
	T66	SW012	U-1262		12.11.90			Switzerland	
	T66	SW013	U-1263		15.01.91			Switzerland	
	T66	SW014	U-1264		07.06.91			Switzerland	
	T66	SW015	U-1265		25.09.91			Switzerland	
	T66	SW016	U-1266		12.04.91			Switzerland	
	T66	SW017	U-1267		12.04.91			Switzerland	
	T66	SW018	U-1268		21.05.91			Switzerland	
	T66	SW019	U-1269		06.06.91			Switzerland	
	T66	SW020	U-1270		31.07.91			Switzerland	
	200	293	ZH200		24.04.87			BAe	
	60A	6Z001	608	18.02.92	19.06.92		ZH570	Zimbabwe	
	60A	6Z002	609		19.06.92		ZH571	Zimbabwe	
	60A	6Z003	610		04.09.92		ZH572	Zimbabwe	
	60A	6Z004	611		04.09.92		ZH573	Zimbabwe	
	60A	6Z005	612		04.09.92		ZH574	Zimbabwe	
	T67	6K001	67-496		08.09.92		ZH593	South Korea	Cr 02.06.94
	T67	6K002	67-497		06.10.92		ZH594	South Korea	
	T67	6K003	67-498		08.09.92		ZH595	South Korea	
	T67	6K004	67-499		10.11.92		ZH596	South Korea	
	T67	6K005	67-500		10.11.92		ZH597	South Korea	Cr 05.01.95
	T67	6K006	67-501		06.10.92		ZH598	South Korea	
	T67	6K007	67-502		06.10.92		ZH599	South Korea	
	T67	6K008	67-503		10.11.92		ZH603	South Korea	
	T67	6K009	67-504		07.12.92		ZH604	South Korea	
	T67	6K010	67-505		22.03.93		ZH605	South Korea	
	T67	6K011	67-506		07.12.92		ZH606	South Korea	
	T67	6K012	67-507		16.02.93		ZH607	South Korea	Cr 05.01.95
	T67	6K013	67-508		16.02.93		ZH608	South Korea	
	T67	6K014	67-509		16.02.93		ZH609	South Korea	

W/N	MARK	LINE NO	SERIAL	FIRST FLT	DELIVERY	REGIST'N	UK SERIAL	CUSTOMER	COMMENTS
	T67	6K015	67-510		23.03.93		ZH610	South Korea	
	T67	6K016	67-511		15.05.93		ZH611	South Korea	
	T67	6K017	67-512		10.05.93		ZH612	South Korea	
	T67	6K018	67-513		02.08.93		ZH613	South Korea	
	T67	6K019	67-514		10.05.93		ZH614	South Korea	
	T67	6K020	67-515		02.08.93		ZH615	South Korea	
	51A	SF001	HW-351		01.10.93		ZH675	Finland	
	51A	SF002	HW-352		06.11.93		ZH699	Finland	
	51A	SF003	HW-353		22.01.94		ZH700	Finland	
	51A	SF004	HW-354		23.03.94		ZH701	Finland	
	51A	SF005	HW-355		21.10.94		ZH702	Finland	
	51A	SF006	HW-356		20.06.94		ZH703	Finland	
	51A	SF007	HW-357		01.09.94		ZH704	Finland	
	102	AT001	1051		20.05.93		ZH621	Abu Dhabi	
	102	AT002	1052		20.05.93		ZH622	Abu Dhabi	
	102	AT003	1053		14.06.93		ZH623	Abu Dhabi	
	102	AT004	1054		22.07.93		ZH624	Abu Dhabi	
	102	AT005	1055		20.05.93		ZH625	Abu Dhabi	
	102	AT006	1056		14.06.93		ZH626	Abu Dhabi	
	102	AT007	1057		20.05.93		ZH627	Abu Dhabi	
	102	AT008	1058		22.07.93		ZH628	Abu Dhabi	
	102	AT009	1059		30.03.94		ZH629	Abu Dhabi	
	102	AT010	1060		22.07.93		ZH634	Abu Dhabi	
	102	AT011	1061		12.11.93		ZH635	Abu Dhabi	
	102	AT012	1062		10.09.93		ZH636	Abu Dhabi	
	102	AT013	1063		10.09.93		ZH637	Abu Dhabi	

The first Hawk T67 67-496 delivered to the Republic of Korea, on 8 September 1992, was unfortunately lost in an accident on 2 June 1994. BAe/CHRIS RYDING

W/N	MARK	LINE NO	SERIAL	FIRST FLT	DELIVERY	REGIST'N	UK SERIAL	CUSTOMER	COMMENTS
	102	AT014	1064		12.11.93		ZH638	Abu Dhabi	
	102	AT015	1065		12.11.93		ZH639	Abu Dhabi	
	102	AT016	1066		23.12.93		ZH640	Abu Dhabi	
	102	AT017	1067		30.03.94		ZH641	Abu Dhabi	
	102	AT018	1068		23.12.93		ZH642	Abu Dhabi	
	103	OT001	101		07.12.93		ZH669	Oman	
	103	OT002	102		14.02.94		ZH670	Oman	
	103	OT003	103		18.01.94		ZH671	Oman	
	103	OT004	104		18.01.94		ZH672	Oman	
	203	OS001	121		05.95		ZH710	Oman	
	203	OS002	122		28.10.94		ZH711	Oman	
	203	OS003	123		16.12.94		ZH712	Oman	
	203	OS004	124		16.12.94		ZH713	Oman	
	203	OS005	125		15.08.94		ZH714	Oman	
	203	OS006	126		15.08.94		ZH719	Oman	
	203	OS007	127		15.08.94		ZH720	Oman	
	203	OS008	128		14.02.95		ZH721	Oman	
	203	OS009	129		28.10.94		ZH722	Oman	
	203	OS010	130		15.08.94		ZH729	Oman	
	203	OS011	131		05.95		ZH730	Oman	
	203	OS012	132		05.95		ZH731	Oman	
	108	MT001	M40-01		14.03.94		ZH735	Malaysia	
	108	MT002	M40-02		14.02.94		ZH738	Malaysia	
	108	MT003	M40-03		14.03.94		ZH745	Malaysia	
	108	MT004	M40-04		11.04.94		ZH746	Malaysia	
	108	MT005	M40-05		11.04.94		ZH747	Malaysia	
	108	MT006	M40-06		11.04.94		ZH748	Malaysia	

The first of Omans' Hawk Mk 103s (101) was delivered on 7 December 1993. BAe/CHRIS RYDING

W/N	MARK	LINE NO	SERIAL	FIRST FLT	DELIVERY	REGIST'N	UK SERIAL	CUSTOMER	COMMENTS
108	MT007	M40-07		09.95			ZH752	Malaysia	
108	MT008	M40-08		27.05.94			ZH753	Malaysia	
108	MT009	M40-09		27.05.94			ZH754	Malaysia	
108	MT010	M40-10		25.07.94			ZH757	Malaysia	
208	MS001	M40-21	04.04.94	25.07.94			ZH778	Malaysia	
208	MS002	M40-22		19.08.94			ZH779	Malaysia	
208	MS003	M40-23		19.08.94			ZH780	Malaysia	
208	MS004	M40-24		22.09.94			ZH781	Malaysia	
208	MS005	M40-25		22.09.94			ZH782	Malaysia	
208	MS006	M40-26		22.09.94			ZH783	Malaysia	
208	MS007	M40-27		17.10.94			ZH784	Malaysia	
208	MS008	M40-28		17.10.94			ZH785	Malaysia	
208	MS009	M40-29		15.11.94			ZH786	Malaysia	
208	MS010	M40-30		12.12.94			ZH787	Malaysia	
208	MS011	M40-31		15.11.94			ZH788	Malaysia	
208	MS012	M40-32		13.03.95			ZH789	Malaysia	
208	MS013	M40-33		12.12.94			ZH790	Malaysia	
208	MS014	M40-34		16.01.95			ZH791	Malaysia	
208	MS015	M40-35		16.01.95			ZH792	Malaysia	
208	MS016	M40-36		13.03.95			ZH793	Malaysia	
208	MS017	M40-37		05.95			ZH794	Malaysia	
208	MS018	M40-38		13.03.95			ZH795	Malaysia	
T63C	63C001	1017		21.02.95			ZH817	Abu Dhabi	
T63C	63C002	1018		21.02.95			ZH818	Abu Dhabi	
T63C	63C003	1019		03.04.95			ZH819	Abu Dhabi	
T63C	63C004	1020		03.04.95			ZH820	Abu Dhabi	
102D	K359	ZJ100	29.02.92					BAe Warton	Demonstrator
200RDA	360	ZJ201	13.02.92					BAe Warton	Demonstrator

Hawk 200 RDA demonstrator ZJ201 was first flown on 13 February 1992. BAe

McDonnell Douglas T-45 Goshawk

MARK	SERIAL	CODE	FIRST FLT	DELIVERY	OPERATOR/UNIT/BASE	COMMENTS
YT-45A	162612				McDonnell Douglas	Cancelled
YT-45A	162613				McDonnell Douglas	Cancelled
T-45A	162787	1	16.04.88		McDonnell Douglas	Cr Edwards AFB - 04.06.92
T-45A	162788	2	02.11.88		McDonnell Douglas/NATC	
T-45A	163599	3	10.10.90		McDonnell Douglas/NATC	
T-45A	163600	[B-200]	15.11.90		USN TW-2, Kingsville, TX	
T-45A	163601	[B-201]	16.12.91	23.01.92	USN TW-2, Kingsville, TX	
T-45A	163602	[B-202]	03.92		USN TW-2, Kingsville, TX	
T-45A	163603	[B-203]	04.92		USN TW-2, Kingsville, TX	
T-45A	163604	[B-204]	05.92		USN TW-2, Kingsville, TX	
T-45A	163605	[B-205]	10.92		USN TW-2, Kingsville, TX	
T-45A	163606	[B-206]	11.92		USN TW-2, Kingsville, TX	
T-45A	163607	[B-207]	12.92		USN TW-2, Kingsville, TX	
T-45A	163608	[B-208]	12.92		USN TW-2, Kingsville, TX	
T-45A	163609	[B-209]	12.92		USN TW-2, Kingsville, TX	
T-45A	163610	[B-210]	04.93		USN TW-2, Kingsville, TX	
T-45A	163611	[B-211]	05.93		USN TW-2, Kingsville, TX	
T-45A	163612	[B-212]	04.93		USN TW-2, Kingsville, TX	
T-45A	163613	[B-213]	05.93		USN TW-2, Kingsville, TX	
T-45A	163614	[B-214]	05.93		USN TW-2, Kingsville, TX	
T-45A	163615	[B-215]	07.93		USN TW-2, Kingsville, TX	
T-45A	163616	[B-216]	06.93		USN TW-2, Kingsville, TX	
T-45A	163617	[B-217]	07.93		USN TW-2, Kingsville, TX	
T-45A	163618	[B-218]	07.93		USN TW-2, Kingsville, TX	
T-45A	163619	[B-219]	09.93		USN TW-2, Kingsville, TX	
T-45A	163620	[B-220]	08.93		USN TW-2, Kingsville, TX	
T-45A	163621	[B-221]	08.93		USN TW-2, Kingsville, TX	
T-45A	163622	[B-222]	08.93		USN TW-2, Kingsville, TX	
T-45A	163623	[B-223]	10.93		USN TW-2, Kingsville, TX	
T-45A	163624	[B-224]	10.93		USN TW-2, Kingsville, TX	

T-45A Goshawk 163636 was delivered to TW-2 at Kingsville in March 1994. PETER R MARCH

MARK	SERIAL	CODE	FIRST FLT	DELIVERY	OPERATOR/UNIT/BASE	COMMENTS
T-45A	163625	[B-225]	10.93		USN TW-2, Kingsville, TX	
T-45A	163626	[B-226]	10.93		USN TW-2, Kingsville, TX	
T-45A	163627	[B-227]	10.93		USN TW-2, Kingsville, TX	
T-45A	163628	[B-228]	11.93		USN TW-2, Kingsville, TX	
T-45A	163629	[B-229]	12.93		USN TW-2, Kingsville, TX	Cr 17.08.94 - coll with 163639
T-45A	163630	[B-230]	12.93		USN TW-2, Kingsville, TX	
T-45A	163631	[B-231]	01.94		USN TW-2, Kingsville, TX	
T-45A	163632	[B-232]	01.94		USN TW-2, Kingsville, TX	
T-45A	163633	[B-233]	02.94		USN TW-2, Kingsville, TX	
T-45A	163634	[B-234]	02.94		USN TW-2, Kingsville, TX	
T-45A	163635		12.93		McDonnell Douglas	Cockpit 21 Demonstrator
T-45A	163636	[B-236]	03.94		USN TW-2, Kingsville, TX	
T-45A	163637	[B-237]	03.94		USN TW-2, Kingsville, TX	
T-45A	163638	[B-238]	04.94		USN TW-2, Kingsville, TX	
T-45A	163639	[B-239]	04.94		USN TW-2, Kingsville, TX	Cr 17.08.94 - coll with 163629
T-45A	163640	[B-240]	05.94		USN TW-2, Kingsville, TX	
T-45A	163641	[B-241]	06.94		USN TW-2, Kingsville, TX	
T-45A	163642	[B-242]	07.94		USN TW-2, Kingsville, TX	
T-45A	163643	[B-243]	08.94		USN TW-2, Kingsville, TX	
T-45A	163644	[B-244]	09.94		USN TW-2, Kingsville, TX	
T-45A	163645		10.94		USN TW-2, Kingsville, TX	
T-45A	163646		12.94		USN TW-2, Kingsville, TX	
T-45A	163647		03.95		McDonnell Douglas	Inlet Fuel Development Aircraft
T-45A	163648		03.95		USN TW-2, Kingsville, TX	
T-45A	163649		03.95		USN TW-2, Kingsville, TX	
T-45A	163650		04.95		USN TW-2, Kingsville, TX	

To be followed by 163651 - 163658 and 165057 - 165092.

A dawn line-up of Goshawks at NAS Kingsville in autumn 1994. MDC

APPENDIX E
UK HAWKS 1995

RAF/RN/MoD(PE) HAWKS (current May 1995)

SERIAL	MARK/CODE	OPERATOR/BASE
XX154	T1 [1]	MoD(PE), T&EE Llanbedr
XX156	T1	MoD(PE), A&AEE Boscombe Down
XX157	T1A	RN FRADU, Yeovilton
XX158	T1A	RAF
XX159	T1A [PA]	RAF No 4 FTS/19(R) Sqn, Valley
XX160	T1	MoD(PE), T&EE Llanbedr
XX161	T1 [DQ]	RAF No 4 FTS/208(R) Sqn, Valley
XX162	T1	MoD(PE) IAM, Boscombe Down
XX164	T1	RAF No 4 FTS, Valley
XX165	T1 [869]	RN FRADU, Yeovilton
XX167	T1 [Q]	RAF No 4 FTS/74(R) Sqn, Valley
XX168	T1	RAF No 6 FTS, Finningley
XX169	T1	RAF No 6 FTS, Finningley
XX170	T1	MoD(PE), T&EE Llanbedr
XX171	T1 [DW]	RAF No 4 FTS/208(R) Sqn, Valley
XX172	T1	RAF St Athan Station Flight
XX173	T1	RAF No 6 FTS, Finningley
XX174	T1	RAF No 6 FTS,Finningley
XX175	T1 [861]	RN FRADU, Yeovilton
XX176	T1 [DS]	RAF No 4 FTS/208(R) Sqn, Finningley
XX177	T1 [CP]	RAF No 4 FTS/74(R) Sqn, Valley
XX178	T1 [M]	RAF No 4 FTS/19(R) Sqn, Valley
XX179	T1 [E]	RAF No 4 FTS/74(R) Sqn, Valley
XX181	T1 [CB]	RAF No 100 Sqn, Finningley
XX183	T1 [868]	RN FRADU, Yeovilton
XX184	T1	RAF St Athan Station Flight
XX185	T1	RAF No 6 FTS, Finningley
XX186	T1A	RN FRADU, Yeovilton
XX187	T1A	RAF No 6 FTS, Finningley
XX188	T1A [CG]	RAF No 100 Sqn, Finningley
XX189	T1A	RAF No 4 FTS/74(R) Sqn, Valley
XX190	T1A	RAF No 4 FTS/74(R) Sqn, Valley
XX191	T1A [DT]	RAF No 4 FTS/208(R) Sqn, Valley
XX193	T1A [TT]	RAF No 4 FTS/74(R) Sqn, Valley
XX194	T1A [TI]	RAF No 4 FTS/74(R) Sqn, Valley
XX195	T1 [CA]	RAF No 100 Sqn, Finningley
XX196	T1A [DB]	RAF No 4 FTS/208(R) Sqn, Valley
XX198	T1A [DC]	RAF No 4 FTS/208(R) Sqn, Valley
XX199	T1A [TG]	RAF No 4 FTS/74(R) Sqn, Valley
XX200	T1A [CF]	RAF No 100 Sqn, Finningley
XX201	T1A [N]	RAF, stored Shawbury
XX202	T1A [P]	RAF, stored Shawbury
XX203	T1A [PC]	RAF No 4 FTS/19(R) Sqn, Valley
XX204	T1A [H]	RAF No 4 FTS, Valley
XX205	T1A [V]	RN FRADU, Yeovilton
XX217	T1A	RAF, stored Shawbury
XX218	T1A	RAF No 4 FTS/74(R) Sqn, Valley
XX219	T1A	RAF, stored Shawbury
XX220	T1A [PD]	RAF No 4 FTS/19(R) Sqn, Valley
XX221	T1A [DG]	RAF No 4 FTS/208(R) Sqn, Valley
XX222	T1A [TJ]	RAF No 4 FTS/74(R) Sqn, Valley
XX224	T1 [PM]	RAF No 4 FTS/19(R) Sqn, Valley

Colourful Hawk T1 XX172 operated by RAF St Athan, the Hawk maintenance unit. PETER R MARCH

Hawk T1 XX185 is flown by No 6 FTS for navigator training.
PETER R MARCH

Range of markings at No 4 FTS Valley – XX225 in the former T1 standard training red/white/blue; XX220 in the TIA air defence grey and XX236 overall black, the new standard scheme for all RAF training Hawks. BAe/GEOFF LEE

XX235 and XX244, the two RAF display Hawk T1s from No 4 FTS, specially painted for the 1995 season. BAe/GEOFF LEE

SERIAL	MARK/CODE	OPERATOR/BASE
XX225	T1 [PN]	RAF No 4 FTS/19(R) Sqn, Valley
XX226	T1 [74]	RAF No 4 FTS/74(R) Sqn, Valley
XX227	T1A	RAF *Red Arrows*, Scampton
XX228	T1 [CC]	RAF No 100 Sqn, Finningley
XX230	T1A	RAF, stored Shawbury
XX231	T1W	RAF No 4 FTS/19(R) Sqn, Valley
XX232	T1	RAF No 6 FTS, Finningley
XX233	T1	RAF *Red Arrows*, Scampton
XX234	T1 [872]	RN FRADU, Yeovilton
XX235	T1	RAF No 4 FTS/74(R) Sqn, Valley
XX236	T1 [PK]	RAF No 4 FTS/19(R) Sqn, Valley
XX237	T1	RAF *Red Arrows*, Scampton
XX238	T1	RAF No 6 FTS, Finningley
XX239	T1 [PL]	RAF No 4 FTS/19(R) Sqn, Valley
XX240	T1	RAF No 6 FTS, Finningley
XX242	T1 [865]	RN FRADU, Yeovilton
XX244	T1	RAF No 4 FTS/74(R) Sqn, Valley

SERIAL	MARK/CODE	OPERATOR/BASE
XX245	T1 [866]	RN FRADU, Yeovilton
XX246	T1A	RAF, stored Shawbury
XX247	T1A [CM]	RAF No 100 Sqn, Finningley
XX248	T1A [CJ]	RAF No 100 Sqn, Finningley
XX249	T1	RAF No 4 FTS/No 19(R) Sqn, Valley
XX250	T1	RAF No 6 FTS, Finningley
XX252	T1A	RAF *Red Arrows*, Scampton
XX253	T1A	RAF *Red Arrows*, Scampton
XX254	T1A	MoD(PE), BAe Brough
XX255	T1A [TE]	RAF No 4 FTS/74(R) Sqn, Valley
XX256	T1A	RAF, stored Shawbury
XX258	T1A [PE]	RAF No 4 FTS/19(R) Sqn, Valley
XX260	T1A	RAF *Red Arrows*, Scampton
XX261	T1A	RAF No 4 FTS/19(R) Sqn, Valley
XX263	T1A	RN FRADU, Yeovilton
XX264	T1A	RAF *Red Arrows*, Scampton
XX265	T1A [CN]	RAF No 100 Sqn, Finningley

Latest colours and markings for No 4 FTS: TIA XX190 No 74 (R) Squadron; T1 XX239 No 19 (R) Squadron and T1 XX290 No 208 (R) Squadron. BAe/GEOFF LEE

The all-black colour scheme was adopted for all RAF training Hawks in 1994. BAe/GEOFF LEE

SERIAL	MARK/CODE	OPERATOR/BASE
XX266	T1A	RAF *Red Arrows*, Scampton
XX278	T1A	RAF No 4 FTS/19(R) Sqn, Valley
XX280	T1A [DJ]	RAF No 4 FTS/208(R) Sqn, Valley
XX281	T1A [O]	RAF No 4 FTS, Valley
XX282	T1A	RAF, stored Shawbury
XX283	T1 [DY]	RAF No 4 FTS/208(R) Sqn, Valley
XX284	T1A [CL]	RAF No 100 Sqn, Finningley
XX285	T1A [CH]	RAF No 100 Sqn, Finningley
XX286	T1A [DK]	RAF No 4 FTS/208(R) Sqn, Valley
XX287	T1A	RAF
XX288	T1W [DX]	RAF No 4 FTS/208(R) Sqn, Valley
XX289	T1A [CI]	RAF No 100 Sqn, Finningley
XX290	T1 [DV]	RAF No 4 FTS/208(R) Sqn, Valley
XX292	T1W [R]	RAF *Red Arrows*, Scampton (on loan)
XX294	T1	RAF *Red Arrows*, Scampton
XX295	T1 [DW]	RAF No 4 FTS/208(R) Sqn, Valley
XX296	T1 [DR]	MoD(PE), A&AEE Boscombe Down
XX299	T1W	RAF No 4 FTS/74(R) Sqn, Valley
XX301	T1A	RN FRADU, Yeovilton
XX302	T1A	RAF No 4 FTS/74(R) Sqn, Valley
XX303	T1A [PF]	RAF No 4 FTS/19(R) Sqn, Valley
XX304	T1A (fuselage)	RAF, stored Shawbury

SERIAL	MARK/CODE	OPERATOR/BASE
XX306	T1A	RAF *Red Arrows*, Scampton
XX307	T1	RAF *Red Arrows*, Scampton
XX308	T1	RAF *Red Arrows*, Scampton
XX309	T1	RAF No 6 FTS, Finningley
XX310	T1W	RAF No 4 FTS/19(R) Sqn, Valley
XX311	T1 [867]	RN FRADU, Yeovilton
XX312	T1 [CF]	RAF No 4 FTS/74(R) Sqn, Valley
XX313	T1	RAF No 4 FTS/74(R) Sqn, Valley
XX314	T1	MoD(PE) ETPS, Boscombe Down
XX315	T1A [DA]	RN FRADU, Yeovilton
XX316	T1A [DF]	RAF No 4 FTS/208(R) Sqn, Valley
XX317	T1A	RAF No 4 FTS/208(R) Sqn, Valley
XX318	T1A [PG]	RAF No 4 FTS/19(R) Sqn, Valley
XX319	T1A [TF]	RN FRADU, Yeovilton
XX320	T1A	RAF, stored Shawbury
XX321	T1A [DH]	RAF No 4 FTS/208(R) Sqn, Valley
XX322	T1A [W]	RAF, stored Shawbury
XX323	T1A [TD]	RAF No 4 FTS/74(R) Sqn, Valley
XX324	T1A [DM]	RAF No 4 FTS/208(R) Sqn, Valley
XX325	T1 [CE]	RAF No 100 Sqn, Finningley
XX326	T1A	RAF No 4 FTS/19(R) Sqn, Valley
XX327	T1	MoD(PE) IAM, Boscombe Down
XX329	T1A	RAF No 4 FTS/19(R) Sqn, Valley
XX330	T1A [DE]	RAF No 4 FTS/208(R) Sqn, Valley
XX331	T1A [CK]	RAF No 100 Sqn, Finningley
XX332	T1A [TW]	RAF No 4 FTS/74(R) Sqn, Valley
XX335	T1A [CD]	RAF No 100 Sqn, Finningley
XX337	T1A [K]	RN FRADU, Yeovilton
XX338	T1W [DZ]	RAF No 4 FTS/208(R) Sqn, Valley
XX339	T1 [PJ]	RAF No 4 FTS/19(R) Sqn, Valley
XX341	T1 ASTRA [1]	MoD(PE) ETPS, Boscombe Down
XX342	T1 [2]	MoD(PE) ETPS, Boscombe Down
XX343	T1 [3]	MoD(PE) ETPS, Boscombe Down
XX345	T1A [DJ]	RAF No 4 FTS/208(R) Sqn, Valley
XX346	T1A	RN FRADU, Yeovilton
XX348	T1A [DN]	RAF No 4 FTS/208(R) Sqn, Valley
XX349	T1W	RAF No 4 FTS/74(R) Sqn, Valley
XX350	T1A [TC]	RAF No 4 FTS/74(R) Sqn, Valley
XX351	T1A [DP]	RAF No 4 FTS/208(R) Sqn, Valley
XX352	T1A [CP]	RAF No 100 Sqn, Finningley

Hawk T1 XX242, one of 16 that has replaced Hunters with the RN FRADU at Yeovilton. BAe/PHIL BOYDEN

Hawk T1 XX342 has always served with the ETPS at Boscombe Down. PETER R MARCH

APPENDIX F
T1A CONVERSIONS

RAF Hawk T1 conversions to Hawk T1A

SERIAL	DELIVERED	SERIAL	DELIVERED	SERIAL	DELIVERED	SERIAL	DELIVERED
XX157	18/04/86	XX217	07/04/84	XX265	11/05/84	XX319	21/05/85
XX158	20/03/85	XX218	29/06/83	XX266	30/01/86	XX320	18/06/85
XX159	30/07/84	XX219	23/05/83	XX278	24/06/85	XX321	29/10/85
XX186	05/04/84	XX220	12/03/86	XX279	18/10/83	XX322	19/03/84
XX187	01/06/83	XX221	04/10/83	XX280	18/12/85	XX323	10/07/85
XX188	12/10/84	XX222	25/06/85	XX281	23/10/84	XX324	28/10/83
XX189	29/04/85	XX227	08/01/86	XX282	10/08/83	XX326	22/11/83
XX190	24/02/84	XX230	12/12/84	XX284	29/07/85	XX329	18/02/86
XX191	05/02/86	XX243	07/08/85	XX285	27/03/86	XX330	12/12/83
XX192	28/09/84	XX246	17/09/84	XX286	25/04/84	XX331	03/12/85
XX193	01/12/83	XX247	05/03/85	XX287	16/06/83	XX332	29/10/85
XX194	11/10/83	XX248	04/12/84	XX289	29/10/84	XX333	10/08/84
XX196	05/07/84	XX252	11/07/84	XX297	21/08/85	XX334	31/05/84
XX197	04/01/84	XX253	10/10/84	XX301	31/07/84	XX335	07/02/85
XX198	03/09/84	XX254	02/05/84	XX302	15/05/85	XX337	09/10/84
XX199	02/04/84	XX255	15/08/84	XX303	18/08/83	XX340	14/10/83
XX200	15/07/83	XX256	30/05/86	XX304	12/04/85	XX345	22/01/86
XX201	27/01/84	XX258	26/07/83	XX306	01/12/84	XX346	01/09/83
XX202	13/02/84	XX260	05/02/85	XX315	03/01/85	XX348	21/05/84
XX203	12/01/84	XX261	08/06/84	XX316	22/02/85	XX350	24/09/85
XX204	22/06/84	XX263	03/11/83	XX317	27/03/85	XX351	26/01/84
XX205	12/11/85	XX264	13/04/84	XX318	08/06/83	XX352	17/09/85

HAWK T1A XX255 (converted in 1984) in the special display colours (No 63 Squadron/2 TWU) during 1991. BAe

HAWK T1A XX303 photographed in 1992, painted in No 79 Squadron 75th anniversary markings. BAe

Converted in 1983, Hawk T1A XX263 was operated at RAF Chivenor with No 63 (Shadow) Sqn. BAe

One of the first Hawk T1A conversions, XX318 carries No 234 Squdron's anniversary Welsh Dragon on its fin. ADRIAN SORESON

In grey air defence markings, Hawk T1A XX222 was flown by No 1 TWU/79 Sqn after its conversion in 1985. BAe

Hawk T1As (XX157 and XX289) while being flown by No 7 FTS in the colours of Nos 19 and 92 (Reserve) Sqns in 1992. BAe/GEOFF LEE

APPENDIX G
OTHER UK SERIALS

Other British military serial numbers allocated to Hawks

SERIAL	VARIANT	CUSTOMER/SERIAL
ZA101	BAe Hawk 50/100 (G-HAWK)	BAe Warton
ZB609	BAe Hawk 52	To Kenya as 1001
ZB618	BAe Hawk 53	To Indonesia as LL-5301
ZB622	BAe Hawk 51	To Finland as HW-302
ZD226	BAe Hawk 51	To Finland as HW-305
ZE472	BAe Hawk 63	To UAE Abu Dhabi as 1014
ZF107	BAe Hawk 64	To Kuwait as 140
ZF108	BAe Hawk 64	To Kuwait as 142
ZF627	BAe Hawk 64	To Kuwait as 147
ZG200	BAe Hawk 200	BAe Dunsfold - Crashed 2 Jul 1986
ZG974	BAe Hawk 66	To Switzerland as U-1251
ZH200	BAe Hawk 200	BAe Warton
ZH570	BAe Hawk 60A	To Zimbabwe as 608
ZH571	BAe Hawk 60A	To Zimbabwe as 609
ZH572	BAe Hawk 60A	To Zimbabwe as 610
ZH573	BAe Hawk 60A	To Zimbabwe as 611
ZH574	BAe Hawk 60A	To Zimbabwe as 612
ZH593	BAe Hawk 67	To South Korea as 67-496
ZH594	BAe Hawk 67	To South Korea as 67-497
ZH595	BAe Hawk 67	To South Korea as 67-498
ZH596	BAe Hawk 67	To South Korea as 67-499
ZH597	BAe Hawk 67	To South Korea as 67-500
ZH598	BAe Hawk 67	To South Korea as 67-501
ZH599	BAe Hawk 67	To South Korea as 67-502
ZH603	BAe Hawk 67	To South Korea as 67-503
ZH604	BAe Hawk 67	To South Korea as 67-504
ZH605	BAe Hawk 67	To South Korea as 67-505
ZH606	BAe Hawk 67	To South Korea as 67-506
ZH607	BAe Hawk 67	To South Korea as 67-507

Finnish Hawk 51 with dual serials HW-302 and ZB622, at Dunsfold in 1980. BAe

ZF107 was carried by Kuwait AF MK64 140 for bomb dropping trials. BAe

Painted up with serial ZF627 for a demonstration flight, Hawk 64 147 received its Kuwait AF insignia before delivery in 1986. BAe

The first Swiss Hawk 66 carried the serial ZG974 for weapon trials in the UK. BAe

SERIAL	VARIANT	CUSTOMER/SERIAL
ZH608	BAe Hawk 67	To South Korea as 67-508
ZH609	BAe Hawk 67	To South Korea as 67-509
ZH610	BAe Hawk 67	To South Korea as 67-510
ZH611	BAe Hawk 67	To South Korea as 67-511
ZH612	BAe Hawk 67	To South Korea as 67-512
ZH613	BAe Hawk 67	To South Korea as 67-513
ZH614	BAe Hawk 67	To South Korea as 67-514
ZH615	BAe Hawk 67	To South Korea as 67-515
ZH621	BAe Hawk 102	To Abu Dhabi as 1051
ZH622	BAe Hawk 102	To Abu Dhabi as 1052
ZH623	BAe Hawk 102	To Abu Dhabi as 1053
ZH624	BAe Hawk 102	To Abu Dhabi as 1054
ZH625	BAe Hawk 102	To Abu Dhabi as 1055
ZH626	BAe Hawk 102	To Abu Dhabi as 1056
ZH627	BAe Hawk 102	To Abu Dhabi as 1057
ZH628	BAe Hawk 102	To Abu Dhabi as 1058
ZH629	BAe Hawk 102	To Abu Dhabi as 1059
ZH634	BAe Hawk 102	To Abu Dhabi as 1060
ZH635	BAe Hawk 102	To Abu Dhabi as 1061
ZH636	BAe Hawk 102	To Abu Dhabi as 1062
ZH637	BAe Hawk 102	To Abu Dhabi as 1063
ZH638	BAe Hawk 102	To Abu Dhabi as 1064
ZH639	BAe Hawk 102	To Abu Dhabi as 1065
ZH640	BAe Hawk 102	To Abu Dhabi as 1066

South Korean Hawk 67s, 67-513 and 67-515 carried UK serial numbers ZH613 and ZH615 whilst flying in the UK. BAe/CHRIS RYDING

SERIAL	VARIANT	CUSTOMER/SERIAL
ZH641	BAe Hawk 102	To Abu Dhabi as 1067
ZH642	BAe Hawk 102	To Abu Dhabi as 1068
ZH669	BAe Hawk 103	To Oman as 101
ZH670	BAe Hawk 103	To Oman as 102
ZH671	BAe Hawk 103	To Oman as 103
ZH672	BAe Hawk 103	To Oman as 104
ZH675	BAe Hawk 51A	To Finland as HW-351
ZH699	BAe Hawk 51A	To Finland as HW-352
ZH700	BAe Hawk 51A	To Finland as HW-353
ZH701	BAe Hawk 51A	To Finland as HW-354
ZH702	BAe Hawk 51A	To Finland as HW-355
ZH703	BAe Hawk 51A	To Finland as HW-356
ZH704	BAe Hawk 51A	To Finland as HW-357
ZH710	BAe Hawk 203	To Oman as 121
ZH711	BAe Hawk 203	To Oman as 122
ZH712	BAe Hawk 203	To Oman as 123
ZH713	BAe Hawk 203	To Oman as 124
ZH714	BAe Hawk 203	To Oman as 125
ZH719	BAe Hawk 203	To Oman as 126
ZH720	BAe Hawk 203	To Oman as 127
ZH721	BAe Hawk 203	To Oman as 128
ZH722	BAe Hawk 203	To Oman as 129
ZH729	BAe Hawk 203	To Oman as 130
ZH730	BAe Hawk 203	To Oman as 131
ZH731	BAe Hawk 203	To Oman as 132
ZH735	BAe Hawk 108	To Malaysia as M40-01
ZH738	BAe Hawk 108	To Malaysia as M40-02
ZH745	BAe Hawk 108	To Malaysia as M40-03
ZH746	BAe Hawk 108	To Malaysia as M40-04
ZH747	BAe Hawk 108	To Malaysia as M40-05

Omani Hawk 203 121 carried the serial ZH710 for its first flight from Warton on 11 September 1993. TERRY SENIOR

All Malaysian Hawk 208s carried dual serial numbers for flight testing prior to delivery. BAe

SERIAL	VARIANT	CUSTOMER/SERIAL
ZH748	BAe Hawk 108	To Malaysia as M40-06
ZH752	BAe Hawk 108	To Malaysia as M40-07
ZH753	BAe Hawk 108	To Malaysia as M40-08
ZH754	BAe Hawk 108	To Malaysia as M40-09
ZH757	BAe Hawk 108	To Malaysia as M40-10
ZH778	BAe Hawk 208	To Malaysia as M40-21
ZH779	BAe Hawk 208	To Malaysia as M40-22
ZH780	BAe Hawk 208	To Malaysia as M40-23
ZH781	BAe Hawk 208	To Malaysia as M40-24
ZH782	BAe Hawk 208	To Malaysia as M40-25
ZH783	BAe Hawk 208	To Malaysia as M40-26
ZH784	BAe Hawk 208	To Malaysia as M40-27
ZH785	BAe Hawk 208	To Malaysia as M40-28
ZH786	BAe Hawk 208	To Malaysia as M40-29
ZH787	BAe Hawk 208	To Malaysia as M40-30
ZH788	BAe Hawk 208	To Malaysia as M40-31
ZH789	BAe Hawk 208	To Malaysia as M40-32
ZH790	BAe Hawk 208	To Malaysia as M40-33
ZH791	BAe Hawk 208	To Malaysia as M40-34
ZH792	BAe Hawk 208	To Malaysia as M40-35
ZH793	BAe Hawk 208	To Malaysia as M40-36
ZH794	BAe Hawk 208	To Malaysia as M40-37
ZH795	BAe Hawk 208	To Malaysia as M40-38
ZH817	BAe Hawk 63C	To Abu Dhabi as 1017
ZH818	BAe Hawk 63C	To Abu Dhabi as 1018
ZH819	BAe Hawk 63C	To Abu Dhabi as 1019
ZH820	BAe Hawk 63C	To Abu Dhabi as 1020
ZJ100	BAe Hawk 102D	BAe Warton
ZJ201	BAe Hawk 200RDA	BAe Warton

Malaysian Hawk 208 ZH778 (M40-21) during refuelling trials with RAF VC10 K3 (ZA149) in April 1994.

Fully armed Hawk 200 RDA ZJ201 has been a company demonstrator since it was first flown on 13 February 1992. BAe/GEOFF LEE

On 21st August 1995 the **British Aerospace Hawk** came of age.

The sun continues to rise on this UK aerospace success story, as descendants of the original trainer are developed to meet the requirements of air arms around the world, for the new millenium.

Titles available in this series:-

01 INTERNATIONAL AIR TATTOO 93
The world's largest military airshow
Published October 1993
ISBN 0-9516581-4-X
Price £10.95

02 MIGHTY HERCULES
The first four decades
Published July 1994
ISBN 0-9516581-6-6
Price £14.95

03 INTERNATIONAL AIR TATTOO 94
The best in military aviation
Published October 1994
ISBN 0-9516581-7-4
Price £10.95

04 ROYAL AIR FORCE ALMANAC
A directory of the RAF
Published October 1994
ISBN 0-9516581-8-2
Price £14.95

05 THE REAL AVIATION ENTHUSIAST II
A light-hearted look at the aviation enthusiast
Published June 1995
ISBN 0-9516581-9-0
Price £10.95

06 HAWK COMES OF AGE
21 years of the British Aerospace Hawk
Published July 1995
ISBN 1-899808-00-0
Price £14.95

For postage on the above titles add £1.50 UK; £2.50 Europe; £3 Outside Europe by Surface Mail for each publication.

Also available the special edition
BRACE BY WIRE TO FLY-BY-WIRE
Celebrating the 75th Anniversary of the Royal Force Benevolent Fund
This magnificent book is a tribute to the 75 year history of both the Fund and the Royal Air Force. Fine colour prints by leading aviation artists depict individual years of RAF service, each faced by informative text appropriate to that year.
ISBN 0-9516581-3-1 Hardback – 168pp, sturdy slipcase
Price: £34.95 inc p&p (UK) £36.95 inc p&p (overseas)

These books are available from RAF Benevolent Fund Enterprises Publishing, Building 15, RAF Fairford, Glos GL7 4DL, England. Send IMO or Sterling cheque drawn on UK Bank payable to RAFBF Enterprises or charge made against Visa or Access/Mastercard – please quote Card No, name of bearer and expiry date. Tel: 01285 713300 Fax: 01285 713268